The Life of the Servant

Henry Suso

Translated by

James M. Clark
Formerly Professor of German in the
University of Glasgow

James Clarke & Co
Cambridge

First published 1952
Paperback edition 1982

ISBN 0 227 67862 1

© James Clarke & Co 1952

Published by
James Clarke & Co
7 All Saints' Passage
Cambridge
CB2 3LS
England

Printed and bound in Great Britain by
Redwood Burn Limited, Trowbridge, Wiltshire

TRANSLATOR'S PREFACE

Suso's autobiography is a classic of religious literature, worthy to be placed beside such works as the *Confessions* of St. Augustine or *The Imitation of Christ*. It holds a unique position in the rich and varied productions of the German mystics, since it is the only one in which we hear at first hand the authentic experiences of the author. This cannot be said of the writings of that arch-plagiarist Rulman Merswin, which have, moreover, been very much overrated. Eckhart and Tauler scarcely ever refer to their own experiences. They almost invariably speak with self-effacing objectivity. Suso alone tells us in some detail of his own visions, ecstasies and revelations. His *Life* was never intended for publication, and owes its preservation to an accident. What he confided to his 'spiritual daughter' was meant for her ears alone. In order to console a highly gifted woman in the acute physical sufferings that preceded her death, he told her details of his own life that would otherwise have remained for ever unsaid.

The great value of these utterances lies first in their remarkable sincerity; secondly, in their unsurpassed poetic beauty. They reveal to us a pure and saintly life, lived in the service of a spiritual ideal. Suso was a saint, in the fullest and best sense of the word. He strove with all the energy of an ardent nature to share the life of Christ, both on the physical and on the spiritual plane, to imitate His sufferings, no less than to show forth His divine love and compassion.

Rarely does it happen that such intense spirituality is found combined with such extraordinary literary powers.

Saints are rare enough, but a saint who is also a poet of no mean order is rare indeed. Suso was reared in the home of the *Minnesang*, in the idyllic countryside of his beloved Swabia. He inherited the love of chivalry; he was the scion of a noble house. From his childhood he had heard the songs inspired by that *amour courtois* that had come to Germany from Provence. But instead of singing the praise of an earthly lady, he celebrated a heavenly love, which far surpassed all mundane affection.

He was in many respects a true son of his age. In his veneration of the Virgin and the saints, his theological convictions, his almost incredible austerities, as in so many other ways, his outlook was that of the cloister. But we find also in his writings an element of the universal. Every succeeding generation has found in him a perennial source of inspiration. Protestants and Catholics alike are to be found among his admirers and disciples.

We live in an extremely materialistic age, an age in which the things of the mind and the spirit mean little or nothing to large sections of the community. In common with the best of his contemporaries, Suso saw the world of material things as something transient and deceptive, as compared with the spiritual and invisible world, which was for him the one supreme reality. Here lies the relevance of his works for us to-day. He is the best antidote for soul-destroying materialism.

Suso tells his story, now in homely simple speech, now in the imaginative language of poetry, and without any strict regard for chronology. He briefly characterizes his father as a very worldly man, and his mother as a gentle, pious soul. It was in order to commemorate his mother's name that young Heinrich von Berg assumed her family name of Suso or Süss. Being unable to take part in knightly pursuits because of his frail health, he was sent to the Dominican friary of Constance. His admission before he had attained the prescribed age of fifteen was secured by means of a present, a circumstance which later caused him severe qualms of conscience.[1]

He tells us that his companions in the friary were frivolous and uncongenial: they treated him as a crazy eccentric. There are brief references to his studies at Cologne and the beneficent influence of his wise and saintly master, Eckhart. Suso describes in some detail his severe mortifications of the flesh, and adds that, following a divine command, he finally threw his instruments of torture into the river.

After his first phase as a recluse, which had its vicissitudes of celestial consolation and visitations of doubt or despair, comes the pastoral phase of his life, in which he visited other friaries and convents, ministering to the inmates, preaching, teaching, and giving spiritual guidance to his penitents. In this second period, he suffered physical ills, and later persecution and calumny. He persevered in his efforts, and we know from other sources that he finally reached peace and serenity. In the midst of his troubles he was elected by his brethren Prior of Constance, and acquitted himself well in his onerous office, relying more on prayer than on worldly wisdom.

There are some delightful little stories interwoven in the narrative. Suso is seen to advantage in the tale of his sister, the renegade nun (Chapter XXIV), that of the robber (XXVI), of the wicked woman who slandered him (XXXVIII), the conversion of the frivolous girl (XLII). There may be here and there some slight embellishment of the facts, for literary effect. After all, Suso was not writing a history, but an edifying work, and he would have seen no harm in using a poet's licence.

The supernatural plays a large part in the story, and some critics have taken objection to this. It may be

[1] See below, pp. 64–65.

pointed out that Suso had unquestioning faith in a spiritual order of the world. The miraculous was for him an unchallengeable fact. In every event he saw the hand of God. But that he was not over-credulous, but was quite able to distinguish between fact and fiction, is shown by the story of the bleeding crucifix, concerning which he refused to express an opinion. We may also note how carefully he says: 'It seemed to him in a vision.'

In order to reduce this work to reasonable proportions, some abridgment was necessary. As it happens, the third part of the *Life* consists of 'Maxims', which have no logical connection with the autobiography proper. Moreover, in the other two parts there are occasional moralizing or reflective passages and some repetitions. But no essential trait of Suso has been omitted, and the narrative gains by these excisions in unity and compactness.

With characteristic modesty, Suso never mentions his name in the book. Most of the manuscripts have no title, apart from a rubric that runs, 'This book is called Suso', which means 'This is Suso's book': an evident addition by a later scribe. But in one early manuscript we find the title 'The Life of the Servant', which I have here used. It is not inappropriate, because Suso refers to himself as 'The Servant of Eternal Wisdom', or simply 'The Servant'.

JAMES M. CLARK.

GLASGOW.

CONTENTS

Part Two

PART ONE

Prologue

THERE was once a Preacher[1] in Germany, and he was a Swabian by birth. May his name be written in the book of life! He had the desire to be the Servant of Eternal Wisdom and to be known as such. He became acquainted with an enlightened woman who endured in this world much trouble and suffering.[2] She asked him to tell her something about suffering from his own experience, whereby her suffering heart might take strength, and she continued to ask this for some time.

When he came to see her, she persuaded him to impart to her the nature of his beginning and progress in religion, and the various kinds of trials and sufferings he had had. He related all this to her in spiritual confidence. As she derived consolation and instruction from all this, she wrote everything down for her own benefit and for that of others. But she did so secretly, so that he did not know anything about it.

Later, when he had become aware of this spiritual theft, he scolded her for it, and made her hand over everything to him. He took it and burnt all that she gave him at that time. But when he had also obtained the rest, and was about to proceed in the same manner, he was prevented from doing so by a heavenly message from

[1] That is, a Dominican friar, a member of the Order of Friars Preachers.

[2] Elsbeth Stagel. See below, Chapter xxxiii.

[15]

God. And thus the chapters that follow remained un-
burnt, just as she had written them in her own hand,
for the most part. In addition, some wholesome instruction was added thereto in her name, after her death.

Of the Divine Impression

THE Servant's first beginning in religion[1] took place in
his eighteenth year. And although he had already worn
the religious habit for five of these years, his mind was
not at peace. If God could but keep him from the greatest
sins which might blacken his reputation, it seemed to
him that the number of ordinary sins did not matter at
all. Nevertheless he was at this time in some manner
protected by God, so that he felt dissatisfied with himself,
however much attention he paid to the things that
seemed to him desirable. He often felt that there must be
something else that would bring peace to his wandering
heart, and in his restlessness he felt pain. He always chafed
against this manner of life, yet he could not help himself,
till God of His mercy liberated him by a sudden change.
Men wondered at the sudden alteration that had come
over him. One said this and another said that, but what
had really happened to him no one imagined. For God
had secretly drawn him to Him in divine light, and this
brought about a sudden conversion.

[1] The first of the three stages of the mystic way, which leads to
spiritual perfection.

CHAPTER I

Of the First Trials of a Beginner

WHEN this impression from God had been bestowed upon him, many temptations arose within him, by means of which the foe of his salvation would fain have led him astray. And they were these: the inner impulse which had come to him from God demanded of him a complete renunciation of everything which might come between him and God. Temptation, like a flash, resisted this impulse, saying: 'Change thy mind. It is easy to begin, but toilsome to complete.' The inner voice adduced God's strength and His help. The opposing voice suggested that there was no doubt at all of God's power, but it was questionable whether He wanted to help. But the will of God was clearly made known to him, for God in His mercy had promised by the words of His divine mouth that He would truly help all those who undertake anything in His name.

When grace had conquered in this strife, there came a hostile thought in the guise of a friend, counselling him thus: 'It may be as well that thou shouldst amend thyself, but do not exert thyself too much. Begin in such a moderate way that thou canst carry it through to the end. Eat and drink in a reasonable measure and be comfortable, but at the same time guard against sin. Be in thyself as good as thou wouldst, but do not be so abstemious that people are horrified at the very sight of thee. As people say: "If the heart is good, all is good." Thou canst quite well be cheerful in society, and yet remain a good man at the same time. Other people want to go to heaven too, and yet they do not lead such an austere life.'

In this and similar ways he was sorely tempted, but Eternal Wisdom refuted this false counsel thus: 'He who hopes to catch a slippery eel by the tail, and he who hopes to begin a saintly life with a lukewarm heart, are both deceived. For when they think they have caught it, it escapes. Moreover, he who hopes to overcome a pampered, rebellious body by gentleness, lacks common sense. He who would have the world and yet serve God perfectly, strives to do the impossible and will falsify God's teachings themselves. Therefore, if thou art minded to renounce the world, do it to some purpose.' He was harassed by these temptations for some considerable time; at last he plucked up his courage and turned vigorously away from these things.

Many of his unruly impulses died out as a result of avoiding frivolous society. Now and then he was overcome by weakness, and he went to his friends to ease his mind: but it generally happened that he went to them happily and returned from them sadly, for their conversation and the pastimes in which they indulged made him unhappy, and his ways were insufferable to them. Sometimes when he went to them, they mocked him with scathing words, such as these: One said: 'What strange ways are these of thine!' Another said: 'An ordinary life is the safest after all.' A third said: 'It will end badly in any case.' And thus he was bandied about from one to the other. But he was silent like a dumb man, and thought to himself: 'Alas, dear God! There is no better course than flight. Had I never heard these words, they would not hurt me.'

There was one matter that was a source of painful grief to him: he had no one to whom he could pour out his troubles and who was seeking the same goal as he, and in the same manner. Hence he went about a stranger and unloved, shunning all society with great self-control, but as a result great joy flowed into him later.

CHAPTER II

Of the Supernatural Ecstasy which befell Him

AT the beginning of his life in religion it once happened that on St. Agnes Day,[1] after the midday meal in the refectory, he went into the choir. He was alone there and stood in the lower row at the right hand of the choir. At this time he was very depressed by a great sorrow that weighed down upon him. As he stood there, disconsolate and solitary, he went into an ecstasy and saw and heard what is ineffable. It was without form or shape, and yet it bore within itself all forms and shapes of joyous delight. His heart was hungry and yet satisfied, his mind joyous and happy, his wishes were calmed and his desires had died out. He did nothing but gaze into the brilliant light, in which he had forgotten himself and all things. He did not know whether it was day or night. It was a sweetness flowing out of eternal life, with present, unchanging peaceful feeling. He said then: 'If this is not heaven, I do not know what heaven is, for all the suffering that can ever be put into words, could not enable anyone to earn such a reward and for ever possess it.' This blissful ecstasy lasted perhaps an hour, perhaps only half an hour; whether his soul remained in his body, or was separated from his body, he did not know.[2] When he came to himself he felt just like a man who has come from another world. His body felt such pain in that short

[1] 21st January.   [2] 2 Corinthians, xii, 2.

moment that he thought no one could possibly suffer such pain in so short a time, save in death. He then came to himself in some way or other, and sighed from the depths of his soul, and his body sank to the ground as if in a fainting fit. He cried out in his heart: 'Alas, God, where was I, where am I now?' and said: 'Beloved, this hour can never die in my heart.'

He walked with his body, and no one saw or noticed anything outwardly in him, but his soul and his heart were inwardly full of heavenly wonders. The celestial visions went in and out in his deepest depths, and he felt somehow as if he was hovering in the air. The powers of his soul were filled with sweet heavenly scent just as if one pours a good balsam out of a box, and the box afterwards retains a sweet smell. This heavenly odour remained with him a long time afterwards, and gave him a heavenly longing for God.

CHAPTER III

How He married Eternal Wisdom in a Spiritual Manner

THE course which his life pursued for a long time after, through inner discipline, was nothing but a continual ever-present striving for loving union with Eternal Wisdom. How it first began can be read in his *Little Book of Eternal Wisdom* in German and Latin,[1] which God made through his instrumentality.

From his youth up he had a heart full of love. Now Eternal Wisdom offers itself in the Holy Scriptures very affectionately, as a fair beloved, who adorns herself beautifully in order to be well pleasing to all men,

[1] *Horologium Sapientiae*, the Latin version of Suso's *Little Book of Eternal Wisdom*.

speaking gently in the guise of a woman, in order to incline all hearts to herself. At times she says how false other lovers are, but how full of love and faithfulness she is.

His young heart was drawn to her thereby, and it happened to him as when a panther scatters its sweet fragrance and draws to itself the wild creatures of the forest. She often attracted him and charmed him lovingly to her spiritual love, especially by means of the books which are called *The Books of Wisdom*.[1] When they were read at meals, and he heard the endearments described in them, he felt joy in his heart. Hence he was seized by longing, thinking in his loving heart: 'Thou shouldst just for once try thy fortune and see whether this noble friend, of whom I hear such great wonders related could be thy beloved, for thy young, unruly heart can scarcely endure to be without a special object of love.' So he often meditated about her, thinking of her lovingly, and liking her full well with all his heart and soul.

It chanced one morning, when he was at table, that the wise Solomon called out to her, saying: 'Hear, my son, the wise counsel of thy father. If thou wouldst enjoy love, thou shouldst choose gentle Wisdom as thy dear love; for she gives her lovers youth and strength, nobility and riches, honour and profit, great power and an eternal name. She makes him lovely and teaches him to be chivalrous; she gives him praise before men, and fame with the multitudes; she makes him dear and precious to God and men. By her the world was created, by her the heavens were established and the abyss was founded.[2] He who has her, walks prudently, sleeps peacefully and lives securely.

[1] Proverbs, Song of Songs, Ecclesiastes, Wisdom of Solomon, and Ecclesiasticus.

[2] Proverbs, iii, 19.

As he heard these beautiful words read aloud, his longing heart thought at once: 'Alas, what a beloved is this! If she could but be mine, how well I should then be cared for.' Then strange ideas arose in him, opposing this, and he thought: 'Shall I love what I have never seen, and without knowing what it is? A handful of having is better than a houseful of hoping! He who builds a high house, and he who loves in vain, often wear themselves out for a scanty meal. It would be well to love this noble beloved if she allows her servants to look after their bodies and be comfortable. But now she says: "Good food and strong wine and long sleep, he who wants these things may never win the love of Wisdom."[1] When was ever a servant subjected to such a hard trial for the sake of love?'

A thought from God contradicted this: 'It is an old law that suffering and love go together! There is no one who is a lover who does not also suffer, and every lover is a martyr. Therefore it is not unreasonable that one who aspires so high in love should now and then face adversity. Just consider all the misfortunes and cares that the lovers of this world have to endure, whether they will or no.' By this and the like exhortations he was then once more firmly strengthened to hold out to the end. Such trials came to him frequently. Sometimes he was willing, at other times, however, he allowed his heart to dwell on transient love. But when he had sought peace here and there, he always found something inimical to the whole trend of his desires and consequently he was driven back again.[2]

One day they were reading at table a passage from *The Book of Wisdom*,[3] by which his heart was most deeply moved. She said: 'As the fair rose-tree blooms and the high incense smells pure, and spreads an odour as of un-

[1] Proverbs, xxi, 17.   [2] That is, to faith.

[3] Ecclesiasticus, xxiv, 18–21.

[22]

mixed balsam, I am a blooming sweet-smelling, pure beloved without vexation or bitterness. But all other lovers have sweet words and bitter guerdon; their hearts are nets of death, their hands are fetters of iron, their words are sweetened poison, their pastimes the loss of honour.'[1] Then he thought: 'Indeed, how true it is!' and he spoke to himself boldly: 'Truly, I will be her servant.' And again he thought: 'O God, if I could but once see this love, if I could but once exchange a word with her! Ah, what does the beloved look like, that has so many lovely parts concealed within herself? Is it God or man, woman or man, art or wisdom, or what can it be?'

And as far as he was able to see her with the inner eye, in the interpreted allegories of the Scriptures, she showed herself to him in this manner: she was hovering high above him on a throne of clouds. She shone like the morning star, and burnt like the glowing sun. Her crown was eternity, her garment was blessedness, her words sweetness, her embrace the satisfaction of all desire. She was both far and near, high and low: she was present and yet hidden. She allowed others to associate with her, yet none could grasp her. She towered over the topmost heights of the highest heavens, and touched the deepest chasm of the abyss. She spread herself out powerfully from end to end of the earth, and gently ordered all things.[2] Now when he thought he had a fair maiden before him, he suddenly found a noble youth. At times she appeared as a wise teacher, at times she looked to him like a fair lady-love. She bent down lovingly to him, greeted him smilingly, and said to him kindly: 'Give me thy heart, my son!'[3] He bowed down at her feet and thanked her warmly with a humble heart. This was

---

[1] Ecclesiastes, vii. 27.   [2] Wisdom, viii, 1.

[3] Proverbs, xxiii, 26.

[23]

given to him at that time and more could not be vouch-safed to him as yet.

Later, as he wandered round, lost in thoughts of his best beloved, he would enquire within himself and ask his love-lorn heart: 'Ah, my heart, whence flows love and sweetness and grace? Whence comes all gentleness, beauty, joy of heart and loveliness? Does not everything come from the welling spring of the naked Godhead? Onward then, heart and mind and soul, down into the unfathomable abyss of all lovely things! Who will now forbid me? Ah, I embrace thee to-day as my burning heart desires!' And then it flooded up into his soul, like the original emanation of all good, in which he found spiritually everything that is beautiful, lovely and desir-able: everything was there, as no words can describe it.

Thus he acquired the habit, when he heard songs of praise sung or the sound of a sweet instrument, that his heart and mind were suddenly carried away by a heavenly glimpse of his most beloved from whom all love flows. It cannot be told how often the lovely beloved was embraced and lovingly pressed to his affectionate heart. Often it happened to him as when a mother has her baby in her arms and on her lap as it stretches itself up to find its mother, with its head and the movements of its little body, and shows the joy of its heart by its laughter and play. In the same way his heart stretched out of his body up to joyful communion with the blissful presence of Eternal Wisdom and he was transfused with bliss. He then thought: 'Ah, Lord, if I were married to a queen, my soul would taste bliss. Ah, now thou art the empress of my heart and giver of all grace!'

As a result of this contemplation his face became so happy, his eyes so kind, his heart so jubilant, and all his inner senses sang: 'Above all happiness, above all beauty, I have loved thee, my heart's joy and beauty, for happiness has followed me with thee, and I have possessed all good in and with thee.'[1]

CHAPTER IV

How He wrote the Beloved Name of Jesus on His Heart

AT this time an inordinate fire was sent into his soul, which enflamed his heart with divine love. One day, when he felt it in him, and divine love flamed up within him, he went to his cell, to his secret place of refuge and fell into a loving contemplation, saying: 'Ah, gentle God, could I but devise some emblem of love that would be an eternal token between Thee and me, and a proof that I am Thine, and that Thou art the everlasting love of my heart, a token which no forgetfulness could ever efface.'

In this fervent resolve he threw back his scapular, laid bare his breast and took his style in his hand. He looked at his heart and said: 'Ah, almighty God, give me strength and might to-day to fulfil my desire, for to-day Thou must be engraved in the depths of my heart.' And he set to work, and with his style he pierced the flesh over his heart, pricking backwards and forwards, up and down, till he had drawn the name IHS[2] right over his heart. From the sharp stabs the blood flowed copiously out of the flesh and ran down over his body and down his chest. It was such a lovely sight that in the glow of his love he did not heed the pain much.

When he had done this, he went wounded and bleeding as he was, out of the cell to the pulpit under the crucifix,

[1] Wisdom, vii, 10.

[2] The first two and last letters of the name of Jesus in the Greek alphabet.

and knelt down and said: 'Ah, my Lord and only love of my heart, behold the great desire of my heart! Lord, I cannot imprint Thee more deeply in me: ah, Lord, I pray Thee, bring it about that Thou mayst impress Thyself ever more deeply into the bottom of my heart and so write Thy holy name in me that Thou shalt never more depart from my heart.'

For a long time, I do not know for how long, he went about, wounded by love, till he was healed; and the name IHS remained on his heart, as he had desired. The letters were as broad as the breadth of a smoothed-out blade of grass, and as long as a joint of the little finger. He bore the name thus on his heart until his death, and as often as his heart beat, the name was moved. At first it was quite easy to see. He bore it so secretly, however, that no one ever saw it, except one of his friends, to whom he showed it in pious confidence.

Then later, if any trial came upon him, he just looked at this sweet pledge of love, and the trial was all the easier for him. His soul often said, in a loving conversation: 'Lord, lo, the lovers of this world draw the name of their beloved on their garments. Ah, my love, I have drawn Thee in the fresh blood of my heart.'

Once after matins, when he had come from his prayers, he entered his cell, sat down on his chair and put the book of the old Fathers under his head as a pillow. Then he fell into an ecstasy, and it seemed to him as if a light shone out of his heart. As he looked, a golden cross appeared on his heart, and in it were enchased many precious stones, which shone beautifully together. So the Servant took his cowl and wrapped it over his heart, thinking that the bright light that flowed out would easily be covered, so that it could not be seen. But the penetrating glow burnt with such great glory, however much he hid it, that nothing availed to conceal its powerful beauty.

CHAPTER V

Of the Prelude of Divine Consolation by which God encourages many Beginners

HE was accustomed to go into the chapel after matins, and sit down there in his chair for a short rest—his rest was brief and only lasted until the watchman announced the dawn of day—then he opened his eyes. He fell swiftly on his knees and greeted the bright morning star, the gentle queen of heaven, thinking to himself: as the little birds in the summer salute the dawn of day and welcome it joyfully, so would he salute in joyous desire the light-bearer of eternal day. And he then said the words,[1] not heedlessly, but with a sweet, silent echo in his soul.

Once, as he was sitting at this same hour resting, he heard something resound so sweetly in his mind that his whole heart was moved. While the morning star rose, the inner voice sang with a pure sweet melody the words: 'The morning star Mary has risen to-day.' This hymn resounded with such supernatural power within him that his whole heart was swept away, and he joined in joyfully. When they had finished gladly singing together, an unspeakably sweet embrace was vouchsafed to him, and meanwhile a voice spoke to him: 'The more lovingly thou dost embrace me and the more thou dost kiss me spiritually, the more beautifully and blissfully shalt thou be embraced in my eternal glory.' Thereupon his eyes were opened, the tears flowed down his face, and he saluted the rising morning star, as was his wont.

This greeting was followed by the second morning salutation, also with a *venia*,[2] in honour of the gentle Eternal Wisdom, and with the little prayer of praise,

[1] Of the hymn *Stella Maris*.
[2] A complete prostration on the right side: a Dominican form of devotion.

beginning 'My soul has desired in the night,' which he wrote in *The Little Book of Letters*. Then came the third salutation with a *venia*, in honour of the highest loving seraphic spirit which, in the most glowing fire of love, flames up towards Eternal Wisdom, so that this ardent spirit may make the heart of the Servant fervent in divine love, that it may burn of itself and kindle all men by its loving words and doctrines. This was his daily morning salutation at that time.

Once, on Shrove Tuesday, he had prolonged his prayers until the watchman blew his horn at dawn. Then he thought: 'Sit a little longer before thou dost welcome the bright morning star.' His mind was at peace for a short space, and then the heavenly youths began in a loud voice to intone the beautiful response *Arise and be illuminated Jerusalem*,[1] and it sounded indescribably sweet in his soul. When they had sung a little, his soul was so full of the heavenly melody that his frail body could not bear it any longer. His eyes overflowed, and the fervent tears poured out.

About this time, while he was seated, he had a vision in which he was transported into another land. Then it seemed to him as if his guardian angel were standing very kindly before him at his right hand. The Servant arose quickly, and embraced his beloved angel, and pressed him to his heart, as lovingly as he could, that there might be no barrier between them, as it seemed to him. With a sad voice and weeping eyes, he spoke from a full heart: 'Ah, my angel, whom God the beloved has given me to comfort and protect me, I pray thee by the love thou bearest to God not to leave me.' Then the angel answered and said: 'Dost thou not dare to trust in God? Lo, God has embraced thee so lovingly in His eternity that He will never leave thee.'

[1] Isaiah, lx, 1.

After a time of suffering, it happened early one morning that he was surrounded by the heavenly host in a vision. Then he requested one of the bright princes of heaven to show him what God's hidden dwelling-place in his soul looked like. Then the angel said to him: 'Now cast a joyful glance into thyself, and see how God is caressing thy loving soul.' Swiftly he looked in and saw that his body above his heart was clear as crystal; and he saw in the midst of his heart Eternal Wisdom sitting peacefully, in a lovely form, and beside her sat the soul of the Servant, in heavenly longing. She was leaning lovingly at the side of God and His arms held her embraced and pressed to His divine heart. Thus she lay, entranced and in an ecstasy of love in the arms of God the beloved.

Afterwards on the feast of All Angels, he once spent many hours contemplating the bliss of heaven. When day approached, there came to him a youth, who seemed to be a heavenly minstrel sent to him by God. With him there came I know not how many noble youths of the same appearance and bearing as the first; only the former had more dignity, as if he were an archangel. This youth came up to him very cheerfully and observed that they had been sent to him by God, so that they might bring him heavenly joy in his sorrows. He said also that he was to put his sufferings out of his mind and keep company with them and dance with them in a heavenly manner. They led the Servant by the hand to the dance, and the youth struck up the joyous little hymn on the Infant Jesus that runs *In dulci jubilo*.[1] When the Servant heard the beloved name of Jesus so sweetly resound, his heart and soul were so cheerful that all thought of suffering disappeared. He looked on with joy while they made the highest wildest leaps and bounds. The precentor knew

[1] An ancient Christmas carol, written partly in Latin and partly in German.

quite well how to lead the dance; he sang first and they followed. They sang and danced with jubilant hearts. The precentor sang the refrain three times: *Ergo merito*.

The dance was not like those that are danced in this world. It was like a heavenly flowing forth and back again into the lonely abyss[1] of the divine mystery. This and the like celestial consolations were given him countless times in those days, and chiefly at the time when he was beset by great sufferings. These then became all the easier to bear.

CHAPTER VI

Of Various Visions

AT this time he often had visions of future and hidden things, and God allowed him, as far as it was possible, to see clearly what it looks like in heaven and hell and purgatory. Many souls appeared to him when they had departed from this world, to make known to him how it fared with them, and how they had deserved their punishment, how they might be helped, or what their reward from God was.

Among others the blessed Meister Eckhart[2] appeared to him and the saintly friar Johannes der Fuoterer of Strasbourg.[3] He was told by the Master that he (Eckhart) lived in transcendant glory in which his purified soul was glorified in God. Hence the Servant wanted to know two things from him: one was how those persons rest in

[1] The mystics often refer to God in such terms.

[2] The greatest of German mystics. He died in 1329 or earlier, and this vision probably occurred soon after his death. *Meister* is the equivalent of the Latin *Magister*.

[3] A Dominican friar who came of a merchant family in Strasbourg. His name occurs in a document dated 1325. He was famous as a preacher.

God who through true self-surrender without any false-ness, strive to attain divine truth. Then he was shown that no one can put into words how these men are transported into the formless abyss. He asked, however, in addition, what was the most profitable exercise for a man who would fain achieve this. Then the Master said: 'He should die to himself and to his selfhood in true self-surrender. He should accept all things from God and not from creatures, and in quiet patience he should endure in the face of all wolfish men.'

The other friar, Johannes, showed him also in a vision the lovely beauty in which his soul was glorified. The Servant asked if he might put a question to him. It was this: he asked which of all ascetic practices was the one that was most painful to men and yet the most profitable for them? Then Friar Johannes said that there is nothing more painful or more profitable for men than that, when they feel abandoned by God, they should surrender their own wills, and thus forsake God for the sake of God.[1]

His own father, who had been a child of the world, appeared to him after his death, and showed him the lamentable spectacle of his dreadful purgatory. He also explained how he had above all deserved this and told him in detail how he (the Servant) was to help him. This he did. And he showed himself later to the Servant and said that he had been liberated from his afflictions.

His blessed mother, through whose heart and body God had wrought miracles in her lifetime, also appeared in a vision and showed him the great reward that she had received from God. The same thing happened to him from countless other souls: he derived joy therefrom and it often gave him a model to follow and a support in the way of life he then led.

[1] To acquiesce in the sense of God's absence, in order to fulfil His will.

[*31*]

CHAPTER VII

The Rules He observed at Table

WHEN he was about to go to table, he knelt in deep contemplation of Eternal Wisdom in his heart, and begged her very devotedly to go with him and dine with him, saying: 'Most sweet Jesus Christ, I invite Thee with the great desire of my heart, and pray that, just as Thou dost most gently feed me, Thou mayest to-day graciously bestow Thy presence upon me.'

When he sat at table, he placed the beloved guest of pure souls just in front of him as his neighbour, and looked at Him in a very friendly fashion; at times he leaned towards the side of His heart. At every dish that was put before him, he offered his plate to his heavenly Host, asking Him to bless it, and he often spoke in loving friendship: 'Ah, gentle companion, eat now with me; Lord, now help Thyself and eat with Thy servant.' And he used many such words as these.

When he was about to drink, he raised the cup and first offered it to Him to drink. In those days he usually drank five times at table, in rememberance of the five wounds of his dear Lord, but as water and blood ran out of His divine side, he took this drink twice. He partook of the first and last mouthful of food in honour of the most loving heart that this earth ever brought forth, and in honour of the most fervent love of the highest spirit of the Seraphim, that this might be fully vouchsafed to his heart. He offered up the food that did not agree with him to be dipped in His heart wounded with blood, in the firm assurance that it could not injure him then.

He was very fond of fruit, but God would not allow it. In a vision he seemed to see someone offer him an apple, saying: 'Take it, this is what thou likest.' The Servant said: 'No, all my delight is in the lovely Eternal Wisdom.'

The other replied that it was not so, and that he was too fond of fruit. The Servant was ashamed of himself and for two years he never touched fruit.

The two years passed, in which he had often longed for fruit, and in the next year the crop failed, so that there was no fruit in the friary. After many a struggle he overcame himself, not wishing to have a different diet at table from the others, and he prayed to God that if it was His will, the Servant might eat fruit. And it came to pass, for when morning came, a stranger arrived, bringing the friary a fair sum in new Pfennige, and he asked that they should buy apples with it. Thus it happened that for a long time they had enough, and so with gratitude he began again to eat fruit.

He divided a large piece of fruit into four quarters: he ate three in the name of the Holy Trinity: the fourth quarter he ate in the same love as that felt by the Holy Mother when she gave her gentle Child an apple to eat. He ate this part unpeeled because little children are accustomed to eat it in this way. From Christmas Day till some time later he did not eat the fourth quarter, but offered it in his imagination to the gentle Mother, that she might give it to her dear Son, then the Servant would do without it for the Child's sake.

CHAPTER VIII

How He celebrated New Year

In Swabia, his native country, it is the custom in some places at New Year's Eve for the youths to wander round in their foolishness to ask for a present. They sing songs, recite beautiful poems, and by their courtly behaviour they endeavour to induce their lady love to give them a bouquet. When he heard of this, it impressed his loving heart so deeply that he also went on New Year's Eve to his eternal Love and asked for a gift. Before dawn he went up to the image of the pure Mother, pressing to her heart her Child, the fair Eternal Wisdom, on her lap. He knelt down and began to sing to himself in quiet sweet tones, first a sequence for the Mother, begging her to allow him to receive a small bouquet from her Child, and if he did not succeed in attaining his object, asking for her help. And in so doing he felt so earnest that the hot tears poured down his face.

When he had finished singing, he turned to the beloved Wisdom, bowed down at her feet and saluted her from the very depths of his heart, praising and glorifying her beauty, her nobility, her high rank, exalting her eternal majesty above all the fair maidens of this earth. And he did so in song and speech, in thought and desire, to the best of his ability. Then in a spiritual manner he wished to be the herald of all love-lorn hearts and to be the minstrel of all loving thoughts, words and feelings, in order that he, her unworthy servant, might be able to praise his noble lady lovingly enough.

And at last he said: 'Ah, Thou art indeed, beloved, my happy Easter, the summer joy of my heart, my sweet hour. Thou art the love that my young heart alone loves and adores, for whose sake it has abjured all earthly love. Let me, dearly beloved, have my reward for this, and permit me to receive a bouquet from Thee! Ah, gentle heart, do it for the sake of Thy divine virtue, of Thy natural goodness, and let me not go away empty-handed this New Year! How well it would become Thee, my sweet beloved! Remember that one of Thy dear servants has told us of Thee, saying that in Thee there is no Yea and Nay, but only Yea and Yea.[1] Therefore, beloved of my

[1] 2 Corinthians, i, 19–20.

heart, send me to-day a lovely Yea in the shape of Thy heavenly grace. As a lovely wreath is given to foolish lovers, may some special grace, some new light, be offered to me as a New Year's gift by Thy fair hand, my gentle beloved. This and the like he did in those days, and he never went away unrewarded.

CHAPTER IX

Of the Words 'Lift up Your Hearts'

HE was asked what he thought about when he sang the Mass and began the preface which precedes the canon of the Mass, with the words 'Lift up your Hearts!' He replied to this question: 'When I sang "Lift up your hearts" in the Mass, it generally happened that grief and desire for God streamed through my heart and soul, and that my heart was carried out of itself. At these times three kinds of lofty, elevating meditations[1] would arise. Sometimes there was one of them, sometimes two, sometimes all three. I was lifted up into God and through me all creatures were also raised up.

'The first illuminating meditation was this: I contemplated in my inner eye myself, with all that I am, body and soul, and all my powers, and placed around myself all the creatures that God ever created in heaven, on earth and in the four elements, each with its particular name, whether it be bird of the air, beast of the forest, fish in the water, leaf and grass of the earth, the countless grains of sand on the sea shore, and moreover, all the tiny drops of water which have ever fallen or still fall as dew, or snow, or rain. I wished that each of them might resound

[1] Or 'intentions'.

[35]

in a sweet instrument, tuned to the innermost melody of my heart and that they might thus be played as a new joyous hymn of praise to my beloved gentle Lord from eternity to eternity.' Then the loving arms of the soul stretched out and extended themselves rejoicingly towards the countless numbers of all these creatures. It was his endeavour to fill them all with zeal, just as a fresh joyous precentor urges the choir to sing joyfully with him and to raise up their hearts to God, singing 'Lift up your hearts.'

'The second meditation was this,' he said. 'I contemplate my heart and all the hearts of men, considering what pleasure and joy, love and peace those taste who give their hearts to God alone; and on the other hand, what injury and suffering, pain and unrest transitory love inflicts on its slaves. Then I called out with great desire to my heart and all other hearts wherever they may be, to all the ends of the earth: "Come, ye imprisoned hearts, away from the narrow bonds of transient love! Come, ye sleeping hearts, away from the death of sin! Come, ye vain frivolous hearts, from the lukewarmness of your idle, careless lives! Raise yourselves up to freedom and return to the loving God. Lift up your hearts!"

'The third meditation was a friendly call to all men of goodwill, who know not self-surrender, who go about restlessly, neither possessing God nor the creatures, because their affections are scattered hither and thither in the world. I called upon them and upon myself, boldly to risk the loss of ourselves by a complete turning away from ourselves and from all creatures!' These were his thoughts at the words 'Lift up your hearts!'

[36]

CHAPTER X

How He celebrated Candlemas

ON Our Lady's Day, Candlemas,[1] he prepared a candle beforehand by three days of prayer for the heavenly Mother in childbed. The candle was wound of three strands: the first in memory of her virgin purity, the second in memory of her boundless humility, the third in memory of her maternal dignity, three virtues in which she surpassed all other human beings. This spiritual candle he prepared beforehand by singing the *Magnificat* three times every day.

When the day of Candlemas came, he went early in the morning, before anyone went into the church, to the high altar, and waited there in his meditations on the Mother in childbed, until she should come with her heavenly treasure. When she approached the outer gate of the city, he ran in the desire of his heart ahead of all others and hastened to meet her, followed by the throng of all godfearing souls. He fell down before her in the road, and begged her to stop for a while with her procession, until he had sung a hymn. Then he struck up and sang in a spiritual and quiet tone so that his lips moved and yet no one heard him speak: 'O Immaculate,' as feelingly as he could. Bowing down deeply before her with deep emotion, he sang the words 'O thou benignant, thou gracious one' praying that she would show her mild grace to a poor sinner. Then he stood up and followed her with his spiritual candle, full of desire that she would

[1] 2nd February: a celebration of the Purification of the Virgin Mary, and the Presentation of Christ in the Temple (Luke, ii, 22–35). It began with the blessing of candles, and included a procession, which ended at the church.

never allow the burning flames of divine love to be extinguished in him.

When he came to the throng of all loving souls, he joined with them in the hymn 'Adorn the bed,' admonishing them to receive the Lord lovingly, and to embrace His Mother fervently, and in this way he led them with praise and song to the Temple.

After that he went before her with loving zeal, before the Mother entered and gave the Child to Simeon. He knelt down before her, praying her to show him the Child and allow him to kiss Him. When she kindly held Him out to the Servant, he spread out his arms into the vastness of the wide world, embracing the beloved one a thousand times. He looked into His pretty eyes, and His small hands, kissing His little mouth and looking at the childlike limbs of the heavenly treasure. Then he raised up his eyes and cried out in his heart with wonder that He who upholds the heavens should be so great and yet so small, so fair in heaven and so childlike on earth. Then occupied himself with Him, as it occurred to him to do, with singing, with tears and spiritual exercises. He then gave Him back to His Mother, and entered the Temple with her, until everything was accomplished.

CHAPTER XI

How He observed Lent

AT the approach of Shrovetide, on the evening when the *Alleluia* ceases to be sung,[1] and the foolish ones of this world begin to make merry, he began to celebrate in his heart a spiritual Shrovetide, and it was in this wise: first he

[1] During Lent, the *Alleluia*, which is a cry of joy, is omitted from the Mass.

meditated on the brief harmful pleasures of the worldly Shrovetide, considering how for some people long sorrow follows short-lived joy. He said a *Miserere*[1] to God for all the sin and dishonour that takes place in this riotous season.[2] This time he called 'The Peasants' Shrovetide,' because they know nothing better. Secondly, he meditated on the prelude to eternity. He considered how God gives heavenly comfort to His elect friends even in this mortal life, and with thankful praise, he thought over what he had himself received, and felt at peace with God.

That evening before compline, he had entered a heated room in order to get warm, for he was cold and hungry. But nothing hurt him as much as the thirst he suffered. And when he saw others eat meat and drink good wine, while he himself was hungry and thirsty, he was overcome by his feelings. He went out and began to lament and to groan from the depths of his heart.

That night he had a vision and seemed to be in a sick-room. Then outside the room he heard someone sing a heavenly hymn; the notes sounded sweeter than any earthly harp has ever sounded. It was as if a twelve-year old schoolboy was singing alone there. Forgetting his hunger, the Servant listened to the sweet notes and said with a fervent heart: 'Ah, who is it that is singing there? I never heard such a sweet tune on earth!'

Then he seemed to see a noble youth standing there; the youth said: 'Thou shouldst know that this tuneful song is meant for thee.' Then the Servant said: 'Alas, God bless me! Ah, heavenly youth, tell him to sing again!' He sang once more and the sound echoed in the air, and he sang three heavenly hymns from beginning to end.

When the singing was ended, the tuneful boy came, as it seemed to the Servant, through the air to the little

[1] Psalm, li, one of the Penitential Psalms.
[2] The Carnival.

window of the room, and handed the youth a pretty little basket through the window. It was full of red fruit, like red ripe strawberries, and they were fine and big. The youth took the basket from the boy, handed it to the friar and said: 'Look, comrade and brother, this red fruit is sent to thee by thy friend and heavenly Lord, the beautiful boy and Son of the heavenly Father, who also sang to thee. Ah, how well He loves thee!'

The friar felt a glow within him, flushed in the face with joy and gladly accepted the basket, saying: 'Ah, blessed is my heart! This is a welcome present from the kind heavenly boy to me: my heart and soul will ever delight in it!' Then he spoke to the youth and the other celestial beings who were there: 'Ah, dear friends, is it not fitting that I should hold this heavenly youth dear? Yes, indeed, I ought to love him and I would fain ever do what I know to be his will.' And he turned to the above-mentioned youth and said: 'Fair youth, am I not right?' The youth smiled kindly and said: 'Yes, thou art right! It is right that thou shouldst love him, for he has loved and honoured thee more than many other men. Therefore hold him dear. And I say to thee: thou must suffer and, moreover, suffer more than many other men. Hold thyself therefore ready.' The Servant said: 'Ah, I will do that right gladly, and I pray thee, help me that I may see Him and thank Him for His fair gift.' Then he said: 'Now come to the window and cast a glance outside.'

He opened the window and saw in front of it the gentlest, most beautiful boy that had ever been seen by mortal eyes. And when he wanted to go to him through the window, the boy turned affectionately to him and bowed kindly with a friendly blessing and disappeared before his eyes. Thus the vision came to an end. When he came to himself again, he thanked God for the good Shrovetide that he had had.

CHAPTER XII

How He celebrated May Day

ON the eve of May Day he generally planted a spiritual May-pole and honoured it for a time once every day. Among all the beautiful branches that ever grew he could not find anything more similar to the beautiful May than the lovely branch of the Holy Cross, whose blossoms are richer in grace and virtue than all the May blossoms that ever grew.

Beneath this May-pole he made six *venias*, every one of which was meant to adorn the spiritual May by means of contemplation with the most beautiful things that the summer could produce. And he spoke and sang to himself in front of the May-pole in the words of the hymn *Hail, Holy Cross,* thus: 'Hail, heavenly May of Eternal Wisdom, on which the fruit of eternal bliss has grown. For thy everlasting adornment I offer to-day, instead of all red roses, my hearty love; in place of all little violets, a humble bow; for all gentle lilies, a pure embrace; for all kinds of gaily coloured and fair flowers, which all heaths and fields, woods or pastures, trees or meadows, have brought forth in this beautiful May, or ever have been or ever will be brought forth, my heart offers a spiritual kiss: for all joyous birds' song which was ever sung on a May branch in care-free style, my soul offers inexhaustible praise; and for all the ornaments with which a May tree was ever adorned in this world, my heart raises to-day a spiritual song and prays thee, blessed May, to help me to praise thee in this short life in such a way that I may enjoy thee, the living fruit, for ever.'

[*41*]

CHAPTER XIII

Of the Sorrowful Way of the Cross, which He walked with Christ when He was led to His Death

First God spoilt him for a long time with heavenly consolations, and he became quite eager to receive them. All that concerned the Deity was pleasurable to him, but when he had to contemplate Our Lord's Passion, and to submit to imitating Him, that was hard and bitter for him. For this reason he was once severely admonished by God, and a voice within him said: 'Dost thou not know that I am the gate,[1] through which all true Friends of God must pass, who wish to come to true blessedness? Thou must break through My suffering humanity, if thou wouldst truly come to My pure divinity.'[2]

The Servant was afraid: this was a hard word for him. Yet he began to take heed of this, however repugnant it was to him. He began to learn things that he did not know before, and he submitted calmly. So he then began, every night after matins, at his usual place—it was in the chapter house—to sink into Christlike sympathy with all that his Lord and his God, Christ, had once suffered. He got up and walked from corner to corner, so that all sloth might fall from him, and that he might cheerfully and bravely persist in his susceptibility to suffering.

He began with Him at the Last Supper, and walked in his steps from place to place, until he brought Him before Pilate. Last he took Him to the court, already condemned, and went with Him on the sorrowful way

[1] John, x, 9.

[2] One of Suso's favourite themes, borrowed from St. Augustine and St. Bernard. It forms the basis of *The Little Book of Eternal Wisdom*.

of the cross, which He walked from the court of judgment as far as the gallows.

And he went the way of the cross in this manner: when he reached the threshold of the chapter-house, he knelt down and kissed the first footprints which He made, when He had been judged, and turned round to go to His death. Then he began to sing the Psalm of Our Lord's Passion: *Deus, Deus meus, respice,*[1] and while singing it, he went through the door into the cloisters.

Then there were four streets that he went through with the Lord: He went through the first street with Him to His death, desiring that he might leave friends and temporal possessions and suffer for His sake wretched grief and voluntary poverty. In the second street he made a resolve to bring himself to renounce ephemeral honour and fame, and to a voluntary contempt of all this world, meditating on the thought that the Lord Himself had become a worm and a reproach to all men.[2] At the beginning of the third street, he knelt down again and kissed the earth, freely surrendering all unnecessary comfort and pampering of the body to share the pain of his delicate body. He imagined to himself, as it is written, how all His strength was dried up,[3] and His nature had perished. And as they drove Him on so cruelly, he considered how justly all eyes should flow over, and all hearts should sigh. Then, when he came to the fourth street, he knelt down in the middle of the road, as if he was kneeling before the gate of the city, through which He must pass, and then he fell down before Him, and kissed the ground, and prayed to Him that He should not go to His death without him, but that he might go close beside Him. And he imagined it all to himself as vividly as he could, and said the little prayer: *Hail, our King, Son of David,* and then let Him pass on.

[1] Psalm, xxii.   [2] Psalm, xxii, 6.   [3] Psalm, xxii, 15.

After that he knelt down once more, facing the gate and greeted the cross with the verse: *Hail, O Cross, our only hope,* and then let it pass by. After this, he knelt before the gentle Mother, who was led past him in unfathomable grief, and he noticed how lamentable she looked, how sadly she bore herself, and he saw her hot tears, wretched sighs, and sorrowful gestures. He greeted her with the words: *Hail, O Queen,* and kissed her footsteps. He then rose quickly and hastened after his Lord, until he came to His side. And the picture was sometimes as vivid as if he were walking beside Him. Then he remembered that when King David was expelled from his kingdom, the bravest knights marched out at his side and stood by him as his friends.[1]

Here he surrendered his will to the will of God, feeling that whatever God did with him, he would accept for His sake. Finally he took out the Epistle that is read in Holy week from the Prophet Isaiah, which runs: 'Lord, who will believe our report?'[2] which so fittingly depicts Our Lord's going to His death. With that he entered the door of the choir, and went up the steps of the pulpit.

When he came to the foot of the cross, where he had once experienced the Hundred Meditations of His Passion,[3] he knelt down and watched them taking off His clothes, and nailing his Lord to the cross in their savage cruelty. Then he did penance, nailing himself with heartfelt love to his Lord on the cross, praying that neither life nor death, neither sorrow nor joy, might ever divide Him from His Servant.

[1] 2 Kings, xv, 15.

[2] Isaiah, liii, 1.

[3] This is the nucleus of Suso's *Little Book of Eternal Wisdom.*

CHAPTER XIV

Of the Useful Virtue that is known as Silence

THE Servant felt in his inmost soul the impulse to acquire sound peace of mind, and it seemed to him that silence might help him to that end. Therefore he kept his tongue in such control that for thirty years he never broke silence at table, except for one occasion, when he was returning from a chapter[1] with many friars on a ship and they ate on board: then he broke it.

To be able the better to control his tongue and to avoid excessive speech, he meditated on three masters: our father St. Dominic, St. Arsenius[2] and St. Bernard. When he wanted to speak, he passed from one to the other in his imagination, asking their permission. And if the time and place were suitable for speech, he had the permission of the first master. If the words to be spoken caused no entanglement with external things, he was allowed by the second; and if it brought no harm within, he felt that he had the permission of all three. Otherwise, he felt it his duty to be silent. When he was called to the gate,[3] he applied himself to these four things: first, to receive all men kindly; secondly, to be brief; thirdly, to dismiss them with comfort; fourthly, to re-enter without attachment to the world.

[1] A General or Provincial Chapter of the Order.
[2] An Egyptian hermit of the fifth century.
[3] Of the friary.

CHAPTER XV

Of the Mortification of the Flesh

In his youth he had a very lively nature. When he came to be conscious of this, and noticed that he was overloaded with high spirits, he felt grief and sorrow. He tried many ruses and severe penance, to make the flesh subject to the spirit. He wore a hair shirt and an iron chain for a long time, till the blood flowed from him like a river, and he had to take it off.

He secretly had an undergarment of hair made and straps in the garment. There were a hundred and fifty sharp nails driven into it, made of brass and sharpened, and all the points of the nails were set towards his skin. He made the garment very narrow and fastened in front so that it fitted very closely to his body, and the sharp nails drove into his flesh. He also made it just long enough to stretch to his navel. He slept in it at night.

In summer, when it was hot and he was very tired and weak from walking, or when he had been to the surgeon for blood-letting, and lay in bondage to pain, tormented by lice, sometimes he lay moaning and complaining to himself, writhing in pain round and round, like a worm that is pricked by sharp needles. He often felt as though he were lying in an ant-heap, in his fear of the vermin. For if he wanted to sleep, or sometimes when he had fallen asleep, they sucked and bit him to their hearts' content. At times he said to God out of the depths of his heart: 'Alas, dear God, what a death is this! Those who are slain by murderers or wild beasts are speedily released, but here I lie among this loathsome vermin, and I am dying, yet I cannot die properly.' And yet the nights were never so long in winter, nor the summer so hot that he desisted from it.

Lest he should have some respite from this torture,

he thought of an additional thing: he bound a piece of a girdle round his throat, and skilfully fastened leather thongs on it. He slipped his two hands in them, locked his arms with two padlocks, and put the keys on a board before his bed, until he got up at matins and unlocked himself. His arms were so stretched up towards his throat on both sides, and the thongs were so tight, that even if the cell had burnt down over his head, he could not have helped himself. He did this until his hands and arms trembled very much from being stretched. Then he bethought himself of something else.

He had two leather gloves made, such as labourers wear when they tear out thorns, and he made a tinsmith fasten small pointed nails round and round them. These gloves he put on at night. When he tried to use his hands in his sleep, he thrust the pointed nails into his chest and scratched himself. He made dreadful scars on his body, as if a bear had scratched him with its sharp claws. The sores festered in the flesh on his arms and on his heart. When they healed after many weeks, he made himself worse by inflicting new wounds.

For some sixteen years he carried on these torturing exercises. Then, when his veins and his physical frame were chilled and deadened, one Whitsunday a host of angels appeared to him in a vision, and announced that God did not wish him to continue. Then he desisted, and threw everything into the river.

CHAPTER XVI

Of the Sharp Cross that He carried on His Back

MORE than all the other exercises, he felt an ardent desire to bear on his body some sign of the sympathy he felt for the painful sufferings of his crucified Lord. So he made himself a wooden cross, as long as a man's span and of the proper breadth. And he hailed thirty iron nails in it in special rememberance of all His wounds and the five marks of His love.[1] He placed this cross on his bare back, between the shoulders on the flesh, and wore it continually, night and day, for eight years in honour of his crucified Lord.

In the last year he also drove seven needles in, so that the points stuck out through the cross and were fixed in it, and he broke away the other end. He bore the wounds of these sharp needles in praise of the piercing grief of the pure Mother of God, in the hour of His lamentable death.

When he first fixed this cross on his naked back, his human nature was afraid and he thought he would not be able to bear it. So he took it off and blunted the sharp nails a little on a stone. Soon he repented of this unmanly weakness, and he sharpened them all again with a file, and put on his cross once more. It chafed his back where it was bony and made it sore and bleeding. Wherever he sat or stood, he felt as if a hedgehog's spines were on him. If anyone accidentally touched him or knocked against his clothes, he was wounded. In order to make this painful cross more bearable, he carved on the back of it the dear monogram IHS.

Once he had not taken good heed, and had taken the hands of two young girls into his own, while they were sitting before all the congregation beside him, without thinking any harm of it. He soon repented this carelessness and he thought that the unbecoming action should be atoned for. When he had left the girls, and entered the chapel, going to his secret place, he struck himself on the back of the cross for this misdeed so that the sharp nails stuck in his flesh. He also put a ban on himself for

[1] The stigmata on hands, feet and side.

this sin, and would not allow himself to go after matins to his accustomed place in the chapter house, where he prayed to the pure heavenly host, which had previously been present to him in his meditations at this spot.

Afterwards, wishing to atone more fully for this misdeed, he timidly ventured in, fell down at the feet of the Judge, and before Him he took a discipline with the cross; then he went in front of each of the saints round and round the walls of the church, and disciplined himself thirty times, till the blood ran down his back. In this way he did bitter penance for the unlawful pleasure he had had.

On St. Clement's Day,[1] when winter begins, he once made a general confession. And at dusk he shut himself in his cell, and undressed himself to his hair undergarment, took out his scourge with the sharp thorns, and beat himself on body, arms and legs, so that the blood ran down, as it does when one is bled by the physician. He struck himself so hard that the scourge broke into three pieces. As he stood there, and saw himself bleeding—it was a most doleful sight—almost like the beloved Christ, when He was savagely scourged, heartfelt tears flowed from pity of himself. He knelt down, naked and bleeding as he was, in the icy air, and prayed to God to efface his sins before His gentle face.

On St. Benedict's Day,[2] on which he was born into this wretched world, he went into his chapel during the collation. He closed the door and undressed as before. He took out his scourge and began to strike himself. A blow chanced to fall upon his left arm, and struck the median vein or another one. The blood sprang out, and flowed in a stream over his foot, through his toes down on to the floor, forming a pool there. His arm swelled up greatly at once, and became bluish. He was too frightened

---

[1] 23rd November. [2] 21st March.

to strike any more. At this time, at this very hour, a saintly maiden called Anna was praying in a castle in another place. It seemed to her that she was transported to the place where he was taking the discipline. Seeing the cruel blows, she was so moved by compassion that she went to him as he raised his arm to strike himself. She warded off the blow, and it fell upon her arm, as it seemed to her in the vision. When she came to herself she found the marks of blood on her arm, as if the scourge had struck her there. For a long time she bore the visible marks with great pain.

CHAPTER XVII

Of His Bed

At that time he happened to find an old thrown-out door. He put it in his cell on his bedstead, and lay on it without any bedclothes. For his comfort he made himself a very thin little mat of reeds. He put it on the door, but it only reached as far as his knees. Under his bed he put as a bolster a sack full of pease-straw and on it a very small pillow. He had not a thread of bed-clothes and he lay at night in the clothes he wore by day, except that he took off his boots and threw a thick cloak over himself.

And so he prepared himself for a miserable bed, for the hard pease-straw lay in lumps under his head; the cross pricked him with the sharp nails on his back; he had thongs on his arms and the hair garment on his hips. The cloak was very heavy and the door hard. So he lay wretchedly, like a log of wood, unable to move. In winter the frost caused him severe pain for when he wanted to stretch out his feet in sleep, they came out on the door and lay there uncovered and chilled. If he drew them under the cloak, and kept them bent, he had cramp in his legs, which hurt him very much. His feet were full of sores, and his legs swelled as if he had dropsy. His knees were covered with blood and scars, his hips full of scratches from the hair garment, his back was wounded by the cross. His body was wasted away from extreme ascetism; his mouth parched by painful thirst; his hands trembled with weakness. And in this torture he spent day and night. Later he retired to a small cell and made the chair on which he sat his bedstead. It was so narrow and so short that he could not stretch out on it. In this hole he lay on the door for some eight years with his accustomed thongs. In addition, for about twenty-five years he had the custom of not entering a room or going near the friary stove to get warm after compline in winter, however cold it was, unless other reasons made it necessary.

In these years he avoided all baths, water baths and sweating baths, to the detriment of his comfort-seeking body. For a long time he ate once a day in summer and winter, and when he fasted he abstained not only from meat, but even from fish and eggs. He practised such poverty that he would not accept or even touch a penny, either with or without permission. He paid such heed to purity that for a long time he would not scratch himself anywhere on his body, except on his hands and feet.

CHAPTER XVIII

How He broke off the Habit of Drinking

ONCE he began the painful practice of allowing himself only a very small measure of drink. Lest he should be inclined to overstep this measure, either at home or away from home, he procured a small jug of the requisite size and carried it with him when he went out. If he was very thirsty, he only allowed himself to cool his dry mouth, as one refreshes a sick patient in his fever.

For a long time he never drank a drop of wine, except on Easter Day, when he did so in honour of the great festival. Sometimes, when he was very thirsty, and in his strictness would not quench his thirst either with water or wine, he looked up piteously to God, Who addressed him inwardly: 'Remember how I went thirsting in the pangs of death, with but a little drop of vinegar and gall, although all the cool springs in the earth were mine!'

At one time, before Christmas, he practised three additional customs. The first was to remain standing before the high altar on the bare stones after matins until daybreak, and this at the time when the nights were very long, and the bell for matins rang very early. The second was not to go either by day or night to any warm place, nor to warm his hands at the glowing coals on the altar.[1] His hands swelled very much because of the cold. After compline he went to sleep on his chair. The third exercise was to abstain from all drink during the day, however thirsty he was, except at table in the morning, and then he was not thirsty. When evening came, however, his whole being craved for a drink, but he crushed it down with bitter pain.

His mouth was as dry as that of a sick man who is stricken with disease. His tongue was so cracked that it did not heal up for more than a year. When he stood there at compline, and the holy water was scattered as usual, he opened his parched mouth thirstily, and gaped in the direction of the sprinkler, in the hope that a little drop of water might fall on his parched tongue, that it might be a little cooled thereby.

At the collation or at dinner, he pushed away the wine

[1] A chafing-dish was placed on the altar at Mass for warming the hands of the celebrant.

from him, and sometimes he raised his eyes, saying: 'Alas, heavenly Father, accept this cool drink as the sacrifice of my heart's blood, and give Thy Son to drink of it in the thirst which He endured when hanging on the cross in the anguish of death.'

Sometimes he went past the well, and looked at the running water in the little basin. Then he would look up to God with a deep sigh. Sometimes, when he could scarcely bear it any longer, he said from the depths of his heart: 'Alas, Eternal God, for Thy hidden judgments! The broad Lake of Constance is so near, and the clear Rhine flows round me,[1] and yet a single drop of water is so precious. What a sad thing it is!'

This continued until the time when the gospel is read which tells how Our Lord changed the water into wine. He was sitting that Sunday[2] at table, sorrowfully, for his thirst was so intense that his food had no taste. After grace was said, he hastened to his chapel, being no longer able to restrain himself, so grievous was his pain. His sufferings broke out and melted into bitter tears. As he stood there, it seemed as if something spoke in his innermost soul: 'Be of good cheer: God will soon delight and comfort thee. Weep not, valiant knight, fare thee well.' These words rejoiced his heart so much that he stopped weeping; yet so great was his pain that he could not really be joyful. As his tears fell down, something within made him smile in expectation of some future divine adventure, which was soon to be sent to him by God.

The same night he had a vision, and thought that Our Lady was coming to him with the dear child Jesus in the form He had when He was seven years old. He bore in His hand a small jug of fresh water. The jug was

[1] The Dominican friary at Constance was on an island. For a time it was used as a factory, now it is an hotel.

[2] Second Sunday after Epiphany.

shining bright and was a little larger than a friary cup. Our Lady took the jug in her hand and offered it to him to drink. He took it and drank thirstily and quenched his thirst to his heart's content.

He was once walking across the fields, and on a narrow path a poor, honourable woman was coming towards him. When the woman approached him, he stepped off the dry path into the mud to let her pass. The woman turned round and said: 'Dear sir, how is it that thou, an honourable lord and priest, dost turn aside so humbly for a poor woman like me, when it is more fitting that I should give way to thee?' Then he said: 'Ah, my dear woman, it is my custom to show respect and honour to all women out of love for the tender Mother of God in heaven.' She raised her eyes and her hands to the heavens and said: 'Now I beg this noble lady that thou mayst never leave this world without receiving from her some special grace, since thou dost honour her through all of us women.' He said: 'May the pure lady of heaven help me to this!'

Soon after this, he took away from table a thirsty mouth, although there had been a great profusion of all kinds of drinks there. When night fell he had a vision: a heavenly female stood before him and said: 'I am the Mother, who gave thee to drink last night out of the jug. As thou art thirsty, I will give thee to drink from compassion.' Then he said quite shyly to her: 'Ah, pure Being, thou hast nothing in thy hand from which thou canst give me to drink.' Then she answered and said: 'I will give thee to drink of the salutory drink that comes out of my breast.' Then he was so afraid that he was unable to reply, knowing himself to be unworthy of it. Thereupon she spoke very kindly: 'As the heavenly treasure, Jesus, is so beautifully hidden in thy heart, and as thy parched mouth has earned it by such a hard struggle, it shall be vouch-

[54]

safed to thee as a special consolation from me.' She added: 'It is not a bodily drink, it is a wholesome spiritual drink of true purity.' So he allowed it to happen, and thought to himself: 'Now thou canst for once drink enough and quench thy thirst completely!' When he had drunk his fill of the heavenly beverage, something remained in his mouth, like a small soft lump. It was white, like manna. He kept it for some time in his mouth as a proof of the truth.

The Servant carried on this strict life of mortification of the outer man, which is here described in part, from his eighteenth to his fortieth year, and as a result his health was undermined. There was nothing in store for him but death, unless he desisted from such exercises. So he gave it up, and God showed him that this severity and all these austerities had been just a good beginning and a breaking down of the outer man. He intended the Servant to press further on by another path if he ever wanted to reach his goal.

CHAPTER XIX

How He was led to the Spiritual School and instructed in the Knowledge of true Self-Surrender

ONCE after matins, the Servant sat in his chair, and as he meditated he fell into a trance. It seemed to his inner eye that a noble youth came down towards him, and stood before him saying: 'Thou hast been long enough in the lower school and hast exercised thyself long enough in it; thou hast become mature. Come with me now! I will take thee to the highest school that exists in the world. There thou shalt learn diligently the highest knowledge, which will lead thee to divine peace and bring thy holy beginning to a blessed fulfilment.' Thereat he was glad and he arose. The youth took him by the hand and led him, as it seemed to him, to a spiritual land. There was an extremely beautiful house there and it looked as if it was the residence of monks. Those who lived there were concerned with the higher knowledge. When he entered he was kindly received and affectionately welcomed by them. They hastened to their master and told him that someone had come who also wished to be his disciple, and to learn their knowledge. He said: 'First I will see him with my own eyes, to see if he pleases me.' On seeing him, he smiled at him very kindly and said: 'Know from me that this guest is quite capable of becoming a worthy master of our high learning, if he will only patiently submit to living in the narrow cage in which he must be confined.'

The Servant turned to the youth who had brought him there and asked: 'Ah, my dear friend, tell me, what is this highest school and what is this learning thou hast spoken of?' The youth replied 'The high school and the knowledge which is taught here, is nothing but the complete, entire abandonment of one's self, that is to say, that a man must persist in self-abnegnation, however God acts towards him, by Himself or by His creatures. He is to strive at all times, in joy and in sorrow, to remain constant in giving up what is his own, as far as human frailty permits, considering only God's praise and honour, just as the dear Christ did to His heavenly Father.'

When the Servant had heard all this, he was well pleased, and he thought he would learn this knowledge, and that nothing could be so hard that he would fail to achieve it. He wanted to live there and find active occupation there. The youth forbade this, however, saying: 'This learning demands unbroken leisure; the less one does here, the more one has done in reality.' He meant that kind of activity with which a man hinders himself, and does not strive purely for God's praise.

After these words the Servant suddenly came to himself, and sat still as he was. He began to think over the words deeply and noticed that they were the pure truths that Christ Himself taught. He then fell into an inner discussion with himself, saying: 'Look carefully into thyself and thou wilt find that thou art still the slave of thyself, and thou wilt observe that in spite of all thy external actions, which indeed thou dost only carry out for thy own reasons, thou art not sufficiently composed to withstand the tribulations that confront thee from without. Thou art still like a timid hare that lies hidden in a bush and starts at every leaf that falls. Thus it is with thee: thou art afraid all thy days of imaginary sufferings that may befall thee. Thou dost turn pale at the very sight of thy adversary. When thou shouldst face them, thou dost flee; when thou shouldst surrender unarmed, thou dost conceal thyself. Then, when praised thou dost smile, when blamed thou dost grieve. It may well be true that thou dost need a higher school.'

CHAPTER XX

Of the Painful Descent

WHEN God had forbidden the Servant to indulge in those external austerities that had endangered his life, his overwrought nature became so glad that he wept for joy. When he thought of his severe bonds and all that he had suffered and struggled for, he said to himself: 'Now, dear Lord, henceforth I will lead a leisurely and free life, and will enjoy myself.' I will quench my thirst

with wine and water, I will sleep on my sack of straw un-
bound. How often have I wished in my grief that before
my death this consolation might be vouchsafed to me by
God! I have tortured myself long enough; it is time for
me to rest now and henceforth.' Such rash thoughts and
imaginings ran through his mind at that time. Alas, once
more he did not know what God had in store for him.

When he had been well at ease for some weeks, thinking such pleasant thoughts, it chanced that he was sitting
on the chair that served as his bed. He was meditating on
the word of truth spoken by suffering Job: 'The life of
man on earth is a warfare.'[1] During this meditation he
fell into a trance and it seemed to him that a fair youth
came in. He was manly in appearance and bore two
knightly boots with him, and armour such as knights are
wont to wear. He went to the Servant, clothed him in
the armour, and said: 'Be a knight! Thou hast hitherto
been a squire and God will now have thee as a knight.'
The Servant looked at himself in the knightly boots and
said in wonderment: 'Ah, God, what has befallen me?
What has become of me? Am I now to be a knight? I
would rather have my ease henceforth.' He said to the
youth: 'Since then God wishes me to become a knight,
I should much prefer to be dubbed a knight in battle in
honourable wise.' The youth turned aside a little; he
smiled and then said: 'Have no care! Thou shalt have
enough fighting! He who would valiantly contend in
the spiritual chivalry of God will have to face much
harder fighting than was ever known in the days of old
by the famous heroes, of whose valiant deeds of chivalry
the world is now wont to tell in song and story. Thou
dost think that God has taken away thy yoke and cast
away thy bonds, and that thou shouldst now take thy
ease, but it is not so yet. God will not take away thy

[1] Job, vii, 1.

[58]

bonds, He will only change them and make them much harder than ever they were before.'

At this the Servant was sore afraid, and he said: 'Ah, Lord of heaven, what dost thou intend to do with me? Am I the only sinner in the world, and is every other man just? Why dost Thou use the rod on me, poor wretched sinner, and spare so many others? From the days of my youth Thou hast done so to me, crucifying my young body with heavy, wearisome days of sickness, and I thought this would suffice!'

He said: 'No, it is not yet enough. Thou must first be tested thoroughly in all respects, if thou wouldst save thy soul.' The Servant said: 'Lord, show me how many sufferings I still have before me!' He answered and said: 'Look up to the heavens. If thou canst count the infinite number of the stars, then thou canst also count the sufferings which await thee in future.' The Servant said: 'Ah, Lord, pray show me the sufferings beforehand, so that I may know them.'

He replied: 'No, it is better for thee not to know them, lest thou shouldst lose heart. Yet among the countless sufferings that are in store for thee, I will only mention three. The first is this: hitherto thou hast only struck thyself with thy own hands, desisting when thou didst wish, and when thou hadst compassion on thyself. I will now take thee away from thyself, and will hand thee over defenceless to strangers. Thou must then experience the public ruin of thy good name in the estimation of some blind persons. Through this tribulation thou shalt suffer more than from the sharp cross on thy wounded back. For by means of thy former mortifications thou wert raised high in the esteem of others, but now thou shalt be struck down and brought to naught.

'The second suffering is this: however many bitter deaths thou hast inflicted on thyself, by the will of God

[59]

one thing has always remained, namely the possession of a gentle, loving nature. But it will come to pass that, in the very places where thou dost look for special love and fidelity, thou shalt find great disloyalty, pain and distress. The suffering will be so manifold that even the people who are most loyal to thee will have to suffer with thee and from pity of thee.

'The third suffering is this: thou hast been hitherto a pampered, spoilt weakling, and hast swum in divine joy like a fish in the sea. I will now snatch this away from thee, and will let thee suffer want and aridity. Thou shalt be forsaken both by God and all the world, openly persecuted by friend and foe alike. In short, all that gives thee joy and comfort must decline, and what is hateful and distasteful to thee, that shall increase.'

The Servant was so afraid at this that his body trembled all over. He sprang up in a rage and fell down on the ground in the form of a cross, with outstretched arms, crying out from the depths of his heart, in a loud voice to God, lamenting and praying, if it might be His will, that God would relieve him of this great grief in His mild fatherly goodness. But if not, that the heavenly will of His eternal order might be fulfilled in him. When he had thus lain for some time in anguish, something spoke in him thus: 'Be of good cheer! I Myself will be with thee, and will help thee to overcome all these calamities by My grace.' He stood up, and committed himself to the hands of God.

When the morning came, he sat after Mass sadly in his cell, thinking over these things. He was cold, because it was winter. Then something said within him: 'Open the window of thy cell, and look out and learn!' He opened it and looked out. Then he saw a dog running about, carrying round a tattered mat in his mouth, and playing with it in a strange fashion. He threw it up, and he threw it down, and tore holes in it. Then the Servant looked up and gave a deep sigh, and a voice spoke within him: 'Just so shalt thou be torn and tugged about in the mouths of thy brethren!' He thought to himself: 'As there is nothing else for it, submit, and see how the mat allows itself to be ill-treated in silence, and do likewise.' He went down and kept the mat for many years as a precious treasure. Whenever he was on the point of breaking out impatiently, he took it out in order to recognize himself in it, and to be silent before all men.

Among other Friends of God who foretold to him his future sufferings, there came to him a high-born, saintly woman who told him that on the festival of the Angels[1] after matins she had prayed to God for him most fervently. Then she had a vision, and she seemed to be taken to the place where the Servant was, and she saw that there was a fair rose-tree above him, which spread far and wide. It was a lovely sight, and was covered with beautiful roses. She looked up at the sky, and it seemed as if the sun was rising already in a cloudless sky, in bright radiance. In the sun's rays there was a fair child with hands outstretched in the form of a cross. She saw that a beam shone out from the sun to the Servant's heart. It was so powerful that all his veins and limbs were aflame. But the rose-tree bent down, and attempted with its thick boughs to intercept the sun's rays shining on his heart. It did not succeed, for the outpouring rays were so strong that they penetrated all the branches, and shone right into his heart. Then she saw the child come forward, proceeding out of the sun. She said to him: 'Ah, dear child, whither wilt thou go?' He said: 'I have so clearly shone through his love-laden heart that a reflexion of the beam should shine from his heart, which will lovingly draw human hearts to me; and the thick rose-tree signifies

[1] 29th September.

[61]

the manifold sufferings that are in store for him. He cannot prevent them from coming; they must be nobly fulfilled in him.'

Since solitude is so helpful for a beginner in religion, he decided to remain more than ten years secluded from all the world in his friary. When he came from table, he shut himself in his chapel, and stayed there. He did not choose to have long talks at the gate, or elsewhere, with women or men, nor even to see them. He gave his eyes a short distance, beyond which they were not allowed to range: and the limit was five feet. He stayed at home all the time, and would go neither into the town nor into the country: he only wanted to live in seclusion. All these precautions availed nothing, for in these years sufferings befell him openly, by which he was so painfully oppressed, that he was an object of pity to himself and to other men.

Thus he shut himself up for ten years without fetters, and forced himself to remain in the chapel. But in order that his captivity might be the easier to bear, he ordered a painter to draw the ancient Fathers[1] and their sayings, and some other devout subjects which stimulate a suffering man to have patience in adversity. But God would not allow him to become too much attached to this plan, because when the painter had drawn the Fathers in charcoal in the chapel, he had eye-trouble so that he could no longer see to paint. So he took his leave, and said the work must wait till he had recovered. The Servant turned to the painter, and asked him how long it would be before he was well. He said 'Twelve weeks.' The Servant bade him place the ladder, which he had thrown down, on the wall, beside the drawings of the old Fathers. He went up the ladder, and passed his hands over the

[1] As we see from Chapter XXXV, Suso means the Desert Fathers, the hermits of the Thebaid.

pictures, and stroked the painter's eyes, saying: 'In the power of God and the sanctity of these old Fathers, I command you, master, to come back to-morrow; and your eyes will be completely cured.' Early next morning he came, cheerful and well, thanking God and the Servant for his recovery. But the Servant gave the credit to the old Fathers, over whose portraits he had passed his hands.

Once he was tempted by a strong desire to eat meat, for he had abstained from it for many years. When he had eaten some meat, and had barely satisfied his craving, he saw in a vision before him an immense infernal being, who spoke the verse: 'While their meat was yet in their mouths,'[1] and with a roaring voice he said to the by-standers: 'This friar has deserved death, and I will give it him.' They would not allow him to do so, but he pulled out a dreadful gimlet, and said to the Servant: 'As I can-not do anything else to thee, I will torture thy body with this gimlet, and drive it into thy mouth so that the pain thou shalt endure is equal to thy pleasure in eating meat.' And with these words he moved the gimlet towards his mouth. Immediately his cheek-bones and his gums swelled, and his mouth became inflamed, so that he could not open it. For some three days he could eat neither meat nor anything else, save what he was able to suck through his teeth.

CHAPTER XXI

Of Inner Sufferings

AMONG his other sufferings there were three inward ones which were very painful at that time. One of them con-sisted in wicked ideas about the faith. Such thoughts as

[1] Psalm, lxxviii, 30.

these occurred to him: how could God become man; and many other such thoughts. The more he struggled against them, the more he grew. God allowed him to be thus tempted for about nine years; his eyes wept, and his heart cried out to God and His saints for help. At last when it seemed to God to be time, He released him entirely therefrom, and gave him great firmness and enlightenment in the faith.

The second inner suffering was inordinate sadness. He continually felt depressed in his heart, as if a mountain lay upon it. This was partly due to the fact that the sudden change in his life[1] was so abrupt that his cheerful disposition was very much afflicted in consequence. This trouble lasted with him for about eight years.

But the third inner suffering was the temptation to fear that his soul would never be saved, however much he did right, and however much he mortified himself. All this would not help him to become one of the saved: everything was lost in advance. With these thoughts he was tormented day and night. When he was going into the choir, or was going to do any other good deed, temptation came, saying sadly: 'What good does it do to serve God? It is nothing but a curse for thee; there is no help for thee. Leave off in good time; thou art lost, whatever thou dost.' Then he thought to himself: 'Ah, poor man that I am, where shall I turn? If I leave the Order, hell will be my portion; but if I remain in it, there is no hope for me. Alas, God, was ever a man in worse case than I?'

This trial came to him from inordinate fear. He had been told that his admission into the Order had taken place by means of the transfer of worldly goods,[2] whence comes the sin which is called simony, that is, the purchase

[1] His conversion, see p. 16.

[2] Suso had entered the friary at the age of thirteen, two years earlier than the permitted age. His entry was procured by a gift.

of spiritual things by temporal ones. He pondered this in his heart, and so he fell into this distress. When this dreadful suffering had lasted about ten years, so that all this time he considered himself to be simply a lost soul, he went to the saintly Meister Eckhart,[1] and confided his sorrow in him. He freed him from it, so that the Servant was released from the pangs of hell, in which he had so long remained.

CHAPTER XXII

How He set out to bring Wholesome Help to His Neighbours

AFTER he had devoted himself for many years to his own religious life, he was impelled by God through manifold revelations to promote the spiritual welfare of his neighbours. There was no end to the number of sufferings that befell him as a result of these good works, though many souls were helped in this way.

God once revealed this to a chosen Friend of God. Her name was Anna, and she was his spiritual daughter. Once in her devotions, she went into an ecstasy, and she saw the Servant saying Mass on a high mountain. She saw an immense host of persons living in him and attached to him. But all were not in the same position: the more each had of God in him, the more they lived in the Servant also; and the more closely they were united to him, the more God had turned to them. She saw how fervently he prayed for them to the eternal God, Whom he held in his priestly hands;[2] and she asked God to explain to her what this vision meant. Thereupon God

[1] See above, p. 30, note 2.
[2] In the form of the consecrated Host.

answered her thus: 'The vast number of these children who cling to him are all the people who are taught by him, who listen to him, confess to him, or are devoted to him in any other way with special affection. He drew them to Me in such a way that I will bring their lives to a good end, and see that they are never to be separated from My joyous countenance. But whatever sufferings may befall him as a consequence of this, he shall be well rewarded by Me.'

Before the above-mentioned noble maiden knew the Servant of Eternal Wisdom, God gave her the inner impulse to see him. It happened once that she was in an ecstasy, and she was told in a vision to go to the place where the Servant was, and see him. She said: 'I do not recognize him in the crowd of the friars.' Then she was told: 'He is easy to recognize among the others: he has a green crown on his head which is adorned round and round with red and white roses interspersed, like a child's chaplet of roses. And the white roses mean his purity, and the red roses his patience in the manifold sufferings which he must endure.'

'Just as the round halo that it is customary to paint round the heads of saints, denotes the eternal bliss which they enjoy in God, similarly the rosy ring denotes the manifold sufferings that the dear Friends of God have to bear, as long as they serve God as His liege knights in this world.' Then, in her vision, the angel conducted her to the place where he was, and she recognized him at once by the rosy ring that he had round his head.

During this time of suffering, his greatest support from within was the diligent aid of the heavenly angels. Once, when he had lost the power of his outer senses, it seemed to him in a vision that he was led to a place where there was a large host of angels. One of them, who was nearest to him, said: 'Stretch forth thy hand and see!'

He put his hand out, and looking, he beheld that from the middle of his palm there sprang a beautiful red rose with green leaves. The rose grew so large that it covered his hands up to his fingers; it was so fair and bright that it gave his eyes great joy. He turned round his hand, this way and that, and there was a lovely sight on both sides of it. He said with great wonder in his heart: 'Ah, dear friend, what does this vision signify?' The youth said: 'It signifies sufferings and sufferings again, and more and more sufferings to follow, which God will give thee. Those are the four roses on both hands and feet.' The Servant sighed and said: 'Ah, gentle Lord, it is a wondrous dispensation of Thy Providence that suffering should cause men such pain, and yet adorn them so beautifully, in a spiritual sense.'

CHAPTER XXIII

Of Manifold Sufferings

ONCE he came on foot to a small town, near which there was a wooden crucifix, covered over by a small shrine, as is the custom in many places. The people believed that many miracles were wrought there; hence they brought wax images and many pieces of wax,[1] and hung them up there in praise of God.

When he came to the crucifix, he went up and knelt down before it. After praying for a time, he stood up and went to the inn with his companion. A little girl had seen him kneel and pray before the crucifix; she was a seven-year-old child. During the night, thieves came to the shrine, broke open the door, and stole all the wax they found there. At daylight the tidings were rapidly spread

[1] *Ex-votos.*

[67]

throughout the town, and reached the citizen who was the guardian of the shrine. He made enquiries to ascertain who had committed the sacrilege. Then the child said she knew quite well who had done it. On being urged to confess, and to denounce the criminal, she said: 'No one but the friar is guilty of the crime,' meaning the Servant, 'for,' she said, 'I saw him yesterday evening kneeling before the crucifix, and then going into the town.'

The citizens accepted this statement of the child as true, and spread the news all round, so that the slander concerning the friar was made known throughout the town, and he was accused of this offence. Many bad opinions of him were current; men said he should be executed as a malefactor. Hearing these stories, he was sore afraid, innocent as he knew himself to be; and deeply sighing he said to God: 'Ah, Lord, as it needs must be that I should suffer, do thou give me ordinary trials that do not affect my good name, and I would bear them gladly. But now Thou dost strike me to the heart with the loss of my reputation, by means of things which cause me the deepest pain.' Then he stayed in the town till the gossip had been dissipated.

In another place it happened that a great outcry was raised about him, which ran through the town and the whole district. For there was a monastery in the town, in which there was a stone crucifix, and it was said to be a life-size image of Christ. Once in Lent fresh blood was found on this crucifix, under the mark of the wound in His side.

The Servant also came running with the others to see the miracle. When he perceived the blood, he stretched out his hand, and received a drop on his finger, and all those who were standing round saw it. Then a great crowd of towns-folk gathered, and they made him stand up before all the people, and say what he had seen and felt. He did so, and told them, but with this reservation, that he did not express any opinion about the question whether the blood had come from God or men. This he left to others to decide.

The news resounded far and wide, and everyone added to it what he thought fit. It was also stated that he himself had pricked his finger and wiped the blood on the crucifix, so that people would think that the image was bleeding spontaneously. They said he had only collected the crowd because of his avarice, in order to get people's money from them. In other places also they uttered such false calumnies about him, that he had to escape from the town by night, and they pursued him, and would have put him to death if he had not got away. They offered large sums for his apprehension, dead or alive. There were many such evil tales. Wherever these stories were bruited about, they were seized upon as if they were true, and his name was covered with abuse and curses. Many dreadful judgments were passed on him.

Yet there were some sensible persons who knew him, and who said that he was innocent. But such people were so savagely attacked that they had to hold their peace and allow him to be reviled. When an honourable citizen's wife of that town heard the painful and unbelievable story of all that the poor man had innocently suffered, she came to him out of compassion with his distress, and advised him to get a sealed document from the town, stating his innocence, and take it elsewhere, for everybody in the town knew him to be blameless. Then he said: 'Alas, dear lady, if this was my only sorrow, and there were none that God intended to impose in future, I would indeed obtain such a written document, but there are so many sufferings that befall me day by day that I must commend the matter to God, and take no action.'

Once he went down to the Netherlands to attend a chapter. Even on his arrival his trials began, because two eminent men travelled thither with him, who were very busy trying to inflict deep sorrow upon him. He was brought to trial, with a trembling heart, and was charged with many offences. One of them was this: they said that he had made books, in which there was false doctrine, by means of which the whole land was being polluted with heretical filth. For this reason they attacked him savagely by word of mouth, and threatened to do him great injury, although God and men knew him to be innocent of the charges.

God was not content with this heavy trial; He made the weight greater. He sent him a sickness on the return journey. The Servant had a high fever and in addition a painful abscess near his heart. Both from the inner complaint and the outer depression, he lay at death's door, and no one expected him to live. His companion looked at him frequently, expecting to see him breathe his last.

In a strange friary he had lain down very wretchedly in bed, unable to sleep during the night because of his severe sickness. And in his thoughts he meditated on the anguish that Christ suffered on the mountain.[1] While thus meditating, he crept from his bed to the chair, that stood beside the bed, and he sat down, not being able to lie down because of the abscess. As he sat there wretchedly, he saw in a vision a large body of the heavenly host coming into his room to comfort him. And the angels began to sing a celestial song, which sounded so sweet in his ears that his whole outlook was changed. As they sang so joyfully, and the sick Servant sat there so sadly, a youth went up to him, and said very kindly: 'Why art thou silent? Why dost thou not join in with us? Dost thou not know full well the heavenly song?' Then the

[1] The Mount of Olives.

Servant answered him, sighing from his sad heart, and saying: 'Ah, dost thou not see how sad I am? When did a dying man ever rejoice? Am I to sing? I am singing a sad song of sorrow. If ever I sang cheerfully, that is over now, for I am now awaiting the hour of my death.' Then the youth spoke very cheerfully: 'Be of good courage,[1] be glad, nothing will befall thee! Thou shalt yet live to sing such a song that God in His eternity will be praised, and many a suffering soul will be comforted thereby.' Meanwhile his eyes filled with tears, and suddenly in that hour, the abscess burst, and he was cured immediately.

When he had returned home again, a pious Friend of God called on him and said: 'Dear master, although you were more than a hundred leagues from me on your journey, your sufferings were present to me. One day I saw with my inner eye the divine Judge sitting on His throne, and with His permission two evil spirits were let loose. They persecuted you by means of those two eminent men who brought these trials upon you. Then I called to God and said: 'Ah, Lord, how canst Thou permit Thy friend to suffer this bitter sorrow?' He answered and said: 'I chose him as My own, so that he might be formed by such sufferings in the image of My only-begotten Son: and yet My justice must punish the great injustice that is being done to him by the early death of the two men who tormented him.' That happened soon afterwards, as was well-known to many people.

[1] Psalm, xxxi, 25.

CHAPTER XXIV

Of the Great Sorrow that came to Him through His Own Sister

THE Servant had a sister who was in the obedience of the religious life.[1] When the friar was staying elsewhere, it happened that she began to slip out of the convent, and to frequent bad company. Once when she had gone away with this company, she came to harm and fell into sin. Owing to the grief and sorrow that fell upon her, she left the community and ran away, he did not know where.

When he returned home, the sad story was whispered about. Someone came to him and told him what had happened. Then he was petrified with grief, and his heart was frozen within him, so that he walked about like a madman. He asked where she was, and where she had gone, but no one could tell him. He thought: 'New grief has come upon thee again! Now do not despair, see if thou canst help this poor lost soul and sacrifice to-day all thy temporal reputation to merciful God. Cast away all human shame. Leap into the deep muddy pool to raise her up.'

When the friars were standing in the choir, and he went past them into the chancel, his face turned pale, and he felt as if his hair was standing on end. He did not dare to visit anyone, for everyone was ashamed of him; and those who had been his friends before fled from him now. When he sought counsel of his friends, they turned away their faces from him with contempt. Then he remembered poor Job, and said: 'Now must God the merciful comfort me, since I am deserted by the whole world.' He

[1] In the Middle Ages 'religious life' usually meant 'life in a monastery or convent.'

asked continually where he could go to hasten after the poor lost soul. At last he was directed to a place, and he went there.

Now it was St. Agnes' Day,[1] and it was very cold. In the night there had been torrential rain, and the streams were swollen. When he was jumping over a stream, he fell into the water from weakness. As soon as he could get up, he did so, and his internal distress was so great that he scarcely heeded the external danger. When he arrived at the place, he was directed to a small cottage. He dragged his weary steps there, entered, and found her there. When he saw her, he collapsed on the bench where she sat, and twice he fell into a fainting fit. When he came to himself again, he took his sister in his arms, and said: 'Alas, my child, alas, my sister, what have I undergone for thee,' and he went on: 'Alas, gentle maiden, St. Agnes, how bitter thy day is for me!' And he sank down once more, and lost consciousness.

Then his sick sister got up, and fell at his feet, and said to him with great bitter tears, in a lamentable tone: 'Ah, my master and reverend father, what a day of lamentation it was that brought me upon this earth, only to lose God, and bring great distress upon you.[2] Therefore there shall be woe and shame, and sighing for my lost heart for ever and evermore. Alas, faithful rescuer of my lost soul, although I am unworthy that you should speak to me or look at me, remember that you can never show in any way more devotion to God, nor act more like Him in your actions towards a poor sinner and an overladen heart. God has made you compassionate to all wretched creatures; how then can you refuse compassion to me, a poor lost sinner, now that I have become an object of

[1] 21st January.

[2] Suso addresses his sister with the familiar 'thou'; she uses the polite plural 'you'.

[73]

pity to God and man, and that my heavy guilt has so quickly and unexpectedly made me contemptible to all men? You seek out what all men spurn and cry shame upon. Although all men are rightly ashamed of me, you face the disgrace, and seek me out. Sir, I adjure you, by my unceasing distress of heart, stretched out and bowed down at your feet as I am, to honour God in me, poor fallen sinner, and forgive me sincerely my crime and my misdeeds, which I have committed against you and against my poor soul. Remember, that if I have dragged your good name and your very life in the mud in this world, you shall receive special honour and eternal consolation for it. And have mercy upon me, poor wretch, who have fallen into the snare, who must always drag my grief with me as my allotted portion in heart and soul, and must ever be a burden to others and to myself. Just let me be, now and then, your lost sister, your new-found and dearly redeemed beggar child. My heart will never again desire so much as to have the right to be your true sister or to be so called. And this resolve is so firm in my heart that if anyone calls me your sister, or if anyone were to point me out as your sister, it would be a great grief to my heart. I shall often feel compassion for you when you are somewhere where I am present, and suffering for me, knowing as I do from what you have said, that a gentle heart cannot fail to be ashamed of all this, and that you have to endure it. And there neither should nor could be any further companionship between us, save that your eyes and ears must be ashamed and frightened of me. I will bear all these enduring ills, and offer them to God for my scandalous sins, that thou mayst obtain mercy and true reformation for me, poor sinner, from God, and help my poor soul to regain grace.'[1]

[1] The disjointed, almost incoherent, language admirably expresses the speaker's agitation.

When the friar had come to himself, he replied to these lamentations thus: 'Alas, hot tears, break out of a full heart that cannot contain itself for grief! Alas, my child, alas, thou only joy of my heart and soul from my childhood's days, in whom I had hoped to have joy and comfort, come here and let me hold thee to the dead heart of thy forlorn brother! Let me shed on my sister's face the bitter tears of my eyes; let me cry and weep over my dead child! Alas, ten thousand deaths of the body is a small evil, but the death of the soul and honour is a great one! Alas for the pain and grief of my wretched heart! Ah, God, merciful God, what have I lived to see! Ah, my child, come here to me! Now that I have found my child, I will cease to lament and weep, and will receive thee today with the same mercy and pity with which the All-merciful God will, I pray, lift me up, poor sinful man, at my latter end. I will freely forgive thee the boundless sorrow and grief that I have had to bear because of thee, and shall bear until my dying day, and I will help thee to atone for thy misdeeds, and to do penance before God and man.' All those who witnessed the scene felt compassion, as they heard the lament of the pair. None could refrain from weeping at the sad sight. Thus, with lamentation and kind consolation, he softened her heart, and she acquired the will to submit again immediately to obedience.

When with indescribable shame, at great cost, and with great effort, he had brought back to the arms of merciful God this lost lamb, God in His mercy ordained that she should be admitted to a convent that was much more reliable than the former one. Afterwards, her zeal for God became so great, and her well-ordered, holy life was so confirmed in virtue until her death, that he was richly rewarded before God and man for all the pain and sorrow he had ever had. When the faithful friar saw that his sufferings had led to such a good end, he had pleasure and joy, and he remembered the hidden order of God, by which all things work together for the good of good men.[1] Then he looked up to God with great gratitude, and his heart welled up in divine praise.

CHAPTER XXV

Of the Deep Sorrow that once came upon Him through One of His Companions

ONCE, when he was about to set out on a journey, a companion was given to him, a lay brother, who was mentally unbalanced. He was reluctant to take him with him, for he recollected what trials he had suffered from his companions in the past. Yet finally he agreed, and took him with him.

Now it happened that they entered a village before breakfast. That day there was a fair, and all kinds of people had come to it. It had been raining, and his companion was wet through; he entered a house and went up to the fire, saying that he could go no further. He told the Servant to do his business without him and said he would wait for him there.

Scarcely had the friar left the house, when his companion got up and sat at the table, joining some rough fellows and traders who had come to the fair. They saw that the wine had gone to his head; so when he got up and stood in the doorway, gaping at them, they seized him and said he had stolen a cheese from them. While these wicked men were brutally ill-treating him, four or five soldiers came up and attacked him, and said that the evil monk was a poisoner of wells. For it was at this

[1] Romans, viii, 28.

time that there were great rumours of poisoning abroad.[1] So they seized him and made such a commotion that many men ran up to the place.

When the lay brother saw how things stood, and that he was a prisoner, he wanted to escape, so he turned round and cried out to them: 'Stop a while, stand still; let me say what I have to say, and I will tell you how it happened, for it is, alas, a sad story!' They stopped, and all listened. He began and said: 'Look and you will all see for your-selves that I am a fool and an ignorant man, and no one pays any attention to me. But my companion is a wise and experienced man. His Order has entrusted to him bags of poison to sink in the wells, here and there in the country as far as Alsace, whither he is now bound. Every-where he goes he will defile everything with deadly poison. See to it that you get him soon, or he will commit crimes that no one can ever undo. He has just taken out a little bag, and he has thrown it in the village well, so that all those who come to the fair, and drink out of the well, will be poisoned. That is why I stayed here, and would not go out, because I do not like it. And as a proof that I am telling the truth, you should know that he has a large sack, which is full of these bags of poison and with the gold pieces, that he and his Order have got from the Jews to pay him for committing these crimes.'

When the wild ruffians who had gathered round heard these words, they raged and cried with a loud voice: 'Come along, away with the murderer before he escapes!' One grasped his pike, another his axe, and each took any weapon he could find, and they ran with wild ferocious gestures. They broke open houses and monasteries, search-ing every place where they thought they might find him, thrusting their naked swords through bedding and

[1] Such rumours were common at the time of the Black Death (1349–50).

[77]

straw, so that the whole fair came running along. People from other towns also came up, honourable men who knew the Servant. When they heard his name mentioned, they came forward and persuaded the mob that they were doing him an injustice, that he was a very pious man, who was incapable of committing such a crime. Not finding him, they finally desisted in their search, and took his companion to the judge as a prisoner. The latter ordered him to be locked up in a cell.

This went on until daybreak. The Servant knew nothing of these disturbances. When he thought it time to break his fast, and he hoped his companion had got dry before the fire, he entered the inn to have a meal. But when he entered the tavern, they began to tell him the whole story of what had happened. He ran forthwith in great alarm to the house where his companion and the judge were, and begged for his companion to be liberated. But the judge said this could not be done: he intended to commit him to prison for his crime. This was sad and doleful news for the Servant, who ran hither and thither to get help. But he could not find anyone who would help him. After carrying on his efforts with great shame and grief, he finally procured the man's release by payment of a heavy fine.

He now thought his troubles were at an end, but they were only just beginning. For when, with pain and loss, he had escaped from the authorities, he fell into danger of his life. For, as he was leaving the judge, about the time of vespers, the rumour had spread among the common people and young boys that he was a poisoner. They denounced him as a murderer, so that he did not dare to leave the town. They pointed at him, and said: 'Look, fellows, that is the poisoner! He has kept out of our way all day; he must be put to death! His money won't help him with us, as it did with the judge!' When he tried to escape down into the village, they cried out all the louder after him. Some said: 'We will drown him in the Rhine,' for this river flowed past the village. Others cried: 'No, the unclean murderer will pollute all the water; we should burn him alive.'

A huge peasant with a sooty jacket grabbed a pike, pushed between the others and cried: 'Listen to me, gentlemen all! We cannot inflict any more shameful death on the wicked heretic than this: I will thrust this long pike through him, as one does to a venomous toad that one impales. Just let me stick this pike through the naked body of this poisoner. I will lift him up from behind, and fix him fast in this fence, and take care that he does not fall. Let his unclean corpse dry in the wind, so that all the people that pass to and fro will have a sight of the murderer, and will curse him after his shameful death, and that he may be all the more accursed both in this world and the next. For the vile scoundrel has well deserved it.'

The wretched Servant heard all this with bitter fear, groaning deeply, and the large tears ran down his face. All those who stood round in a circle, and saw him in his anguish, wept bitterly, and some beat their breasts with compassion, and struck their hands together over their heads. But no one dared to speak, fearing the dreadful rabble would attack them also. At nightfall, he went to and fro, begging with tears that for God's sake someone would have mercy and give him lodging. But he was cruelly driven away. Some kind women would gladly have given him shelter, but they did not dare to do so.

The wretched sufferer was thus in peril of his life, and all human help had deserted him, as everyone was just waiting to see them attack him and kill him. He fell down in anguish and fear of death in front of a fence, raised his wretched swollen eyes to the heavenly Father, saying:

'Alas, Father of all mercies, when wilt Thou come to my aid to-day in my great distress? Alas, merciful heart, why hast Thou forgotten Thy mercy to me? Alas, Father, alas, faithful, mild Father, help me, wretched man, in this great misery! I cannot take counsel with my own heart, since it is dead already, whether it would be more tolerable to drown, or to be burnt alive, or to die at the stake, yet I must suffer one of these deaths. I commend to Thee to-day my wretched spirit. Have mercy on me in the face of the miserable death that threatens me: they are near me who would destroy me.' This sorrowful lament came to the ears of a priest, who ran vigorously to him, dragged him out of their hands, took him to his house and kept him overnight, so that no harm came to him. Early the next morning he helped him to escape from all his troubles.

CHAPTER XXVI

Of the Murderer

ONCE he was journeying from the Netherlands, and going along the banks of the Rhine. He then had a young companion with him, who was able to walk fast. One day it happened that he was not able to keep up with his companion, for he had become very weary and exhausted. His companion was a good half league ahead of him. Then he looked round for someone with whom he could traverse the forest that he had just reached. It was late in the day; the forest was vast and eerie, for many people had been murdered in it. So he stopped at the edge of the forest, and waited for someone to come.

Then two persons came walking along briskly. One

was a young, good-looking woman, the other was a tall, ruffianly looking man, with a spear and a long knife. He wore a black jacket. The Servant was frightened at the fearful ugliness of the man, and looked round to see if he could catch sight of anyone following him. Yet no one was to be seen. Then he thought: 'Alas, Lord God, what strange people these are! How shall I go down through this vast forest and what may befall me to-day?' Then he made the sign of the cross over his heart, and ventured on.

When they had got deep into the forest, the woman came to him, and asked who he was, and what was his name? He told her, and she said: 'Sir, I know you well by name. I beg of you, hear my confession.' She began to confess and said: 'Alas, virtuous sir, I must complain to you, a great wrong has been done to me. Do you see the man who is following us? He is a real murderer, and kills people here in this forest, takes their money and their clothes away, and he spares no one on earth. He has deceived me, and taken me away from my honourable friends, and now I am perforce his wife.'

He was so sore afraid at these words that he almost swooned. He looked round in his distress, to see if anyone was to be heard or seen, or if there was any way of escape. But he neither saw nor heard anyone in the dark gloomy forest, save the murderer at his heels. Then he thought: 'If thou fleest, weary as thou art, he will soon overtake thee and kill thee. If thou criest out, no one will hear thee in this desolate place, and thou wilt likewise be dead.' And he looked up wretchedly and said: 'Ah, God, what will happen to me to-day? Alas, death, alas, death, how near thou art to me!'

When the woman had made her confession, she went back to the murderer, and begged him in a whisper saying: 'O, dear comrade, go and confess also. At home they have great faith in him. They believe that anyone who has confessed to him will never be forsaken by God, no matter how sinful he is. Do so, therefore, and perhaps God will come to thy help at thy last hour for his sake.' As they were whispering together, he was quite terrified, and thought: 'Thou art betrayed!' The murderer came silently forward. When the poor man saw the murderer approaching with his spear, his whole body trembled and was full of fear. He thought: 'Ah, now thou art lost,' for he did not know what they had said to each other.

Now the district was of this nature: the Rhine flowed beside the forest, and a narrow path ran along the bank of the river. The murderer managed to get on the side next to the forest, so that the friar was on the side of the water. As the friar was thus walking on with a beating heart, the murderer began to confess, and told of all the murders and felonies he had ever committed. In particular, he described one horrible murder, that struck terror to the heart of the Servant.

He related: 'Once I went into this forest in order to kill, as I did to-day. I then met an honourable priest, to whom I confessed. He was walking beside me, just as you are doing, and when the confession was made,' he said, 'I drew out this knife, that I carry on me, stabbed him with it, and hurled him away over the bushes into the Rhine.'

At these words and the gestures of the murderer, the Servant turned pale and suffered agonies. The cold sweat ran over his face and down his chest. Struck dumb with fear, his brain reeling, he looked round to see whether the murderer was going to thrust the knife into him and hurl him down also. At last when he was on the point of falling down with fear, and could go no further, he looked back with the air of a man who would fain escape death. The young woman saw his wretched face, ran up

[*82*]

and caught him in her arms as he sank down, supported him firmly, saying: 'Good sir, be not afraid, he will not kill you.' The murderer said: 'I have heard many good things about you. To-day you shall be rewarded for this, for I will spare your life on this account. Pray to God to be merciful to me, poor murderer, at my last breath for your sake.'

Meanwhile they had come out of the forest. His companion was sitting under a tree at the edge of the forest, and was waiting for him. The murderer and the woman went on their way. But the Servant staggered to his companion, and fell to the ground, trembling in his heart and his whole body, as if shaken by a fever, and he lay thus for some time. When he came to himself, he got up and set out on his way, begging God earnestly and with a deep sigh for the murderer, asking that God would reward him[1] for the faith that the murderer had in him, and that God would not suffer him to be damned at his last breath. God answered his prayer in such a way that he could not doubt that the man was to be one of the redeemed, and therefore his soul would never be separated from God.

CHAPTER XXVII

In Perils of Waters[2]

HE was once travelling to Strasbourg, as was his wont. On his return he fell into the Rhine, which had overflowed its banks, bearing with him his new book, which the Evil One hated beyond measure.[3] As he was being

---

[1] The murderer.   [2] 2 Corinthians, xi, 26.
[3] *The Little Book of Eternal Wisdom.*

swiftly carried downstream, helpless and in danger of drowning, a young newly dubbed knight from Prussia[1] chanced to come that way. He boldly plunged into the raging waters, and saved the Servant from death, together with his companion.

Once he was travelling under obedience on a cold day. He had been travelling all day without food until late, in a waggon, in the cold wind and the frosty weather. They came to a dark river, which was deep and swift, being swollen by heavy rain. The labourer who was driving, carelessly went too near the bank, and the waggon was overturned. The friar was thrown from the cart, and fell into the water, lying in it on his back. The waggon followed and fell upon him, so that he could neither turn to the left nor to the right in the water, and could not save himself in any way. Thus man and cart were perforce swept some distance down the river towards a mill. The labourer and other people ran up, sprang into the waves, and seized him with the hope of rescuing him, but the heavy waggon was above him, and kept him down. They pulled the waggon away from him with a great effort, and dragged him to the shore, dripping as he was. When he emerged from the water, his clothes soon froze on him because of the severe cold. He shivered with the frost with chattering teeth, stood there for a while, and then said to God: 'Alas, God, what shall I do, or what shall I attempt to do? It is late at night; and yet there is no town or village near, where I could get warm, or be restored to life. Must I now die here in this way? It would be a lamentable death.'

He looked in every direction, and then he saw far away on a hill-side a very small village; so he crept there, sodden and chilled to the bone. By this time it was late

[1] Young squires used to go to Prussia to join the Crusade against the heathen Slavs, and thus win their spurs in battle.

at night. He went from door to door, asking for a night's lodging in the name of God, but he was driven away from the houses, and no one would take pity on him, Then the cold and weariness began to affect his heart, so that he feared for his life. He called out in a loud voice to God: 'Lord, Lord, Thou shouldst rather have let me drown, then I would at least have been released, rather than that I should die here on this road with cold.' A farmer heard his lamentable words: he was one of those who had driven him away, and he had compassion on him, and he took him in his arms and into his house, where he spent the night in tribulation.

CHAPTER XXVIII

Of a Short Respite that God once vouchsafed to Him

GOD had accustomed him to the thought that, when one trial left him, he would soon be confronted by another. So God tried him without intermission; only once did He allow him to go free and it was not for long. At this time, he had come to a nunnery, and his daughters in religion asked him how things stood with him. He said: 'I fear that things go badly with me, because I have now spent four weeks without ever being attacked in my body or my reputation by anyone, quite contrary to my former custom. Alas, I fear that God has forgotten me.'

When he had been sitting for a short time at the grille of the convent, a friar of his Order came up, called him out, and said: 'Not long ago I was at a castle, and the lord of the castle asked about you angrily, and wanted to know where you were. He also raised up his hand, and swore in the presence of everybody that wherever he found you, he would run a sword through your body. A few reckless warriors swore the same oath; they were his nearest kinsmen, and they have already sought you in some monasteries in the neighbourhood, in order to vent their rage on you. So be warned, and take heed, as you value your life.'

At these words he was afraid, and said to the friar: 'I should like to know what I have done to deserve death.' Then he said: 'This lord had been told that you have turned the head of his daughter, and also of many other persons, and persuaded them to follow a strange manner of life, which they call "the life of the spirit." Those who so live are called "the spirits."[1] He said it had been explained to him that they are the craziest people on earth. And in addition, another man of violence who was there said of you: "He robbed me of a woman who was very dear to me. Now she has taken the veil; she will only look into her own soul. He shall pay for this."' When he heard this news, he said: 'Praise be to God!' and he hastened back to the grille, and said to his daughters: 'Ah, my children, farewell! God has remembered me, and has not forgotten me!' And he told them the harsh words that had been said, and how they wanted to repay his good deeds.

CHAPTER XXIX

Of a Loving Account that He once settled with God

IN those days of pain, and in the places where he then lived, the Servant sometimes went into the hospital, to give his sick body a little respite. When he then sat at

[1] Apparently Suso's spiritual daughters are being confused with a sect known as 'The Brethren of the Free Spirit'.

table, as was his wont, he was sorely tried by mockery and insults. At first it pained him deeply, and he was so grieved that his tears often poured down his cheeks, and ran into his mouth, mixing with his food and drink. Then he looked up silently to God, and said with a deep sigh: 'Ah, God, is it not enough that I should suffer such trials day and night, must even my scanty food at meal-times be mixed with great tribulation?' This often happened to him in full measure.

Once, coming from table, he could control himself no no longer: he went into his secret place, and said to God: 'Ah, dear God and Lord of all the world, be gentle and kind to me, poor man, for to-day I must settle accounts with Thee. I cannot refrain from so doing. Lord, I call Thee to witness, Who knowest all things, have I not had a gentle heart all my days from my mother's womb? I never saw a man in pain or sorrow without sincerely sympathizing with him. I never liked, either in the presence of men or in their absence, to listen to anything that might cause them pain. All my fellows must admit that I have scarcely ever made one of my brethren's reputation worse by my words, either in presence of my superiors or elsewhere. Nay rather, I have endeavoured to make other people's repute better, as far as I could. But if I could not do so I was silent, or I fled, lest I should hear anything. I joined myself all the more closely to those whose honour was impugned, in order that their good name might be more readily restored. I was called the true father of the poor; I was the special friend of all the Friends of God. All who came to see me sad or oppressed, always found a little good counsel with which they went away cheerful and comforted, for I wept with those that sorrowed and mourned with those that mourned,[1] until I took them back home again with

[1] Romans, xii, 15.

a mother's solicitude. However great was the sorrow that anyone caused me, if only he smiled at me kindly, it was all forgotten in the name of God, as if it had never been.

'Lord, I will be silent about mankind, but I will say this: the pain and sufferings of all the little animals and birds and of all God's creatures, if I saw or heard them, they went to my heart. If I could not help them, I sighed with them, and prayed the almighty and most merciful Lord to help them. All that lives on earth obtained mercy and gentleness from me.

'Ah, and Thou, gentle Lord, dost permit some, of whom the dear Paul speaks, whom he calls his false brethren,[1] ah, Lord, I lament that they treat me with such ferocity. Thou knowest, Lord, and it is all apparent to Thee. Ah, gentle Lord, look upon this and requite this to me by the gift of Thyself!'

After he had thus poured out his heart to God for some time, peace came upon him, and words were spoken to him by God: 'Thy childlike reckoning, which thou hast held with Me, arises because thou dost not at all times keep carefully before thee the words and works of the suffering Christ. Know that God is not satisfied with thy kind heart; He wants more from thee. He wants this: if thou art publicly abused by someone by word or deed, thou must not only suffer in patience, thou must also die entirely to thyself, by not going to sleep without first seeking out thy adversaries, and as far as in thee lies, calming their angry hearts by thy sweet humble words and actions. For by such gentle humility thou takest the sword and knife out of their hands, and makest them impotent in their wickedness. Lo, this is the old, the perfect way, that the dear Christ taught His disciples, when He said: 'Behold, I send you out as sheep among wolves.'[2]

[1] 2 Corinthians, xi, 27.   [2] Luke, x, 3.

[88]

When the Servant came to himself, this perfect counsel seemed to him too hard, and it was difficult for him to consider it, and even more so to obey it. And yet he submitted, and began to learn to do it.

Then it once happened that a lay brother, a cobbler, spoke to him very insolently, and insulted him in public. He was quite silent, and wanted to leave it at that. Yet from within he felt that he must do more. When the evening came, and that brother was eating in the hospital, the Servant went to the front of the hospital, and stood waiting until the lay brother came out. When he came out, the Servant fell down before him and said with a humble pleading: 'Ah, virtuous father, honour God in my poor self, and if I have troubled you, forgive me sincerely for God's sake.'

The brother stopped, looked up in surprise, and cried out in a voice broken with sobs: 'Ah, what a wonder is this? You have indeed never done me an injury, no more than to others: I have publicly insulted you with my malicious words. You should forgive me, I beg of you!' And so his heart was comforted, and he gained peace.

CHAPTER XXX

How He once came near to Death in His Sufferings

ONE evening, when he went to bed outside the friary, he was seized by faintness, and felt so weak that he thought he was going to die. He lay quite still, and his pulse had ceased to beat. Seeing this, a faithful kind man who looked after him at that time, whom the Servant had drawn to God, and redeemed with difficulty, ran up to him in pain and grief, and put his hand on his heart to see if he were still alive. But there were no signs of life, and he seemed like a dead man. There was no movement, his face was ashen, and all life seemed extinct, as in a body that is placed on a bier. This lasted as long as it takes a man to walk about a league.

While he thus lay unconscious, his spirit was concerned with nothing but God and the Godhead, the true and the truth in eternal indwelling unity. In fact, he had begun to think of these things before his strength failed him and he fainted. In his mind he began to talk to God, and said:[1] 'Ah, Eternal Truth, whose deep abyss is hidden from all creatures, I, Thy poor Servant, foresee that it is now the end of me, as my failing strength shows. Now, at my last hour, I speak to Thee, Almighty Lord, Whom none can delude nor deceive, since all things are apparent to Thee. Thou alone knowest how things stand between Thee and me. Therefore, I seek Thy grace, loving, heavenly Father, and if ever I have departed at all from the highest truth, blot it out, I pray Thee with Thy precious blood, according to Thy grace and my great need. Ah, kneel down, I beseech you, all saints and especially my gracious Lord, St. Nicholas, lift up your hands and help me to pray the Lord for a good end. Ah, pure, gentle, mild Mother, Mary, stretch out thy hand to me to-day, thy gracious hand. In this last hour receive my trusting soul in thy protection, for thou alone art the comfort and joy of my soul. Ah, merciful Christ, as Thou didst faithfully commend Thy dear disciples to Thy heavenly Father, may my dear spiritual children be commended to thee, so that Thou wilt also vouchsafe to them a good and holy end. Now I take a final leave of all creatures, and turn to the pure Godhead, the prime source of eternal blessedness.'

[1] The final sentence of this chapter suggests that the following words were spoken before the ecstasy.

When he had said these things to himself, he lost consciousness, and fell into the weakness just mentioned. Although he and other men thought that he was lost, he came back to himself. The lifeless heart began once more to beat, and the feeling returned to his weak limbs, and he recovered to such an extent that he was as much alive as before.

CHAPTER XXXI

How a Man should offer up His Sufferings in Praiseworthy Manner to God

ONCE, as the Servant was pondering this wearisome struggle in deep meditation, and perceiving therein the hidden mysteries of God, he turned to God with a deep sigh, and said: 'Ah, gentle Lord, these sufferings I have spoken of are outwardly to be regarded as the sharp thorns which pierce through flesh and bone. Permit, therefore, gentle Lord, that besides the sharp thorns of suffering, some sweet fruit may come forth in the shape of sound doctrine, so that we toilworn men may suffer the more patiently and may offer up our sufferings the more easily to the glory of God.'

He earnestly prayed thus to God for some time, and then it once chanced that he was carried away in himself and beyond himself, and in an ecstasy he heard a sweet voice within him saying: 'I will to-day show thee the high nobility of My sufferings, and show thee how a suffering man should offer up his sufferings in praiseworthy manner to God the beloved.' As a result of these sweet words that were spoken within him, his soul was moved, and in an ecstasy, from the immeasurable fulness of his heart, the arms of his soul were stretched out, as it were, to the remotest ends of the world, to heaven and earth. He thanked God with a boundless heartfelt desire, saying: 'Lord, hitherto I have praised Thee in my writings by praising everything that is joyful or lovely in all Thy creatures. Ah, now I must cheerfully begin a new and strange song of praise that I have never known before, since it has now been revealed to me by suffering. It is this: I wish, from the boundless abyss of my heart, that all the pain and suffering that I ever knew, and all the painful grief of all hearts, the pain of all wounds, the groans of all the sick, the piteous sighs of all sad souls, the tears of all weeping eyes, the wrongs suffered by all oppressed persons, the trials of all indigent widows and orphans, the pangs of all who are hungry and athirst, the blood shed by all the martyrs, the self-conquest of all happy and blooming youth, the painful asceticism of all Friends of God, all the hidden and open pain and sorrow, which I or any other downcast sufferer ever underwent, in body, possessions, reputation, in joy or sorrow, or that any man may have to yet suffer henceforth until the Day of Judgment: that all this may become one song of eternal praise, heavenly Father, an everlasting glory to Thy only-begotten Son, from eternity to eternity. And I, Thy poor Servant, ask to-day on behalf of all suffering men, who perchance by reason of their sufferings are unable to give patient thankful praise to God, that I may be their advocate, that I may on their behalf offer up their sufferings this day by my praise, in whatever manner they have suffered, and offer it up to Thee in their stead, as if I myself alone had suffered it altogether right gladly. I offer it up in their stead to-day to Thy only-begotten Son that He may be praised, and that all sufferers may be comforted, whether they are here, in this vale of tears, or in the world beyond, by Thy strength.'

CHAPTER XXXII

How God in this World compensates a Suffering Man for His Suffering

ONE joyful Easter Day, the Servant felt gladness in his heart, as he was sitting resting for a while, as was his custom. Then he asked God what compensation is received from God in this life by those who for His sake have undergone manifold sufferings.

Then, in an ecstasy, God enlightened him thus: 'Rejoice and be of good cheer, all ye suffering and detached men. Their patience[1] shall be gloriously praised; and just as they have been an object of compassion to many men, so also shall many rejoice with God eternally in their worthy praise and eternal glory. They have died with Me, and they shall also rise again joyfully with Me.'

'I will give them three special gifts: they are so noble that no one can value their worth. The first is this: I will give them their heart's desire in heaven and on earth, so that everything they desire will take place. The second is, that I will give them My divine peace, which neither angels, devils, nor men, nor any creature can take away from them. The third is, that I will kiss them so affectionately and embrace them so lovingly that I shall be they, and they shall be I,[2] and we two shall be united in one for ever. And as long delay pains restless hearts, this love shall not be saved up just for this present hour which only lasts for a single moment, but it is to begin now, and they shall enjoy it for ever, as far as mortal men,

[1] The sudden change from second to third person is in the original.

[2] One hesitates to think that Suso wrote these exact words. See John, xvii, 21–3.

each according to his nature, can bear more or less of it.'

The Servant rejoiced at these glad tidings, and when he had come to himself, he sprang up and laughed heartily, so that it echoed loudly in the chapel in which he was, and he said joyously to himself: 'Let anyone who has suffered come forward and complain! God knows that for myself I vow that I feel as if I had never suffered on earth. I do not know what suffering is, but I do know what bliss and joy is. I am given all I can desire, which many an erring heart must needs lack. What more can I desire?'

Thereupon he turned in his mind to Eternal Truth and spoke thus: 'Ah, Eternal Truth, reveal to me now this hidden mystery, as far as one can express it in words. The truth is so completely unknown to many a blind man.' Then he was inwardly instructed thus: 'Behold, those men, with whom it fares well at the breaking through, which man must undergo, by dying to himself and all creatures, these men (and there are not many of them), are so completely lost in soul and mind in God that, so to speak, they know nothing else of themselves save that they apprehend themselves and all things in their prime origin.

'And for this reason they have as much pleasure and delight in everything that God does, as if God stood apart free and inactive, and had permitted them to carry it out according to their own intention. In this manner they have their heart's desire in themselves, for heaven and earth serve them, and all creatures are obedient to them, each one doing what they do, and leaving undone what they leave. Such men never feel sorrow in their hearts for any cause, by this I mean such pain or grief in the heart from which the will, with prudent deliberation, would like to be released. For, as regards external things, they certainly feel pleasure and pain like other people, in fact sometimes they feel them more deeply than others, because of their refined susceptibility, but these emotions have no permanent place in them. Hence outwardly they stand fast and unmoved. Having died to themselves, they are raised above, as far as is possible, so that their joy is full and unchanging in all things. For in the divine being, into which their hearts have passed, if they have found the right way, there is no place for pain or grief, but only for peace and joy.

'In the same measure as thy own frailty leads thee astray, so that thou dost commit sin, as a result of which, pain and grief rightly come to every man, who indulges therein, to that same extent thou shalt still lack this blessedness. But in so far as thou shalt avoid sin and in this respect thou dost die to thyself, and pass in to that state in which thou canst have neither pain nor suffering, inasmuch as pain is there no longer pain and suffering is no longer suffering, but all things are pure peace, then truly all is well with thee. All this takes place when thy own will is abandoned; for such persons are driven out of themselves by the thirst of longing to the will of God and to His righteousness.

'The will of God tastes so sweet to them and they obtain so much glory from it that everything that God decrees for them makes them so joyous that they neither wish nor desire anything else. This is not to be taken to mean that man is forbidden to ask or pray to God, for it is God's will that prayers should be addressed to Him. It is to be understood in the sense of the lawful outgoing from self-hood into the will of the high Godhead, as has been explained. But here there is a hidden impediment which causes many men to stumble: 'Who knows', they say, 'whether it be God's will?' Behold, God is a cause transcendent over all things, which is more inward and present to everything than that thing can be to itself, and

[95]

against Whose will nothing can subsist nor continue to exist for a moment. Therefore, those who ever strive against God's will and would gladly further their own wills, must feel pain. They have no more peace than is to be had in hell, for they are always in tribulation and sadness. On the other hand, to a liberated spirit, God and peace are ever present, in disagreeable as in pleasant circumstances, for it is He indeed Who does everything, and Who is everything.

'How then can the sight of suffering be hard for them to bear, since they see God in it, find God, carry out God's will, and do not know their own wills? I will say nothing of all the illumination, comfort and divine joy, with which God often upholds His suffering friends in secret. These men are, as it were, in heaven; whatever God does in all His creatures, or refrains from doing, all works for good in them. Thus it is that a man who knows how to suffer properly is rewarded in part for his sufferings in this world, for he gains peace and joy in all things, and after death, eternal life is his portion.' Amen.

PART TWO

CHAPTER XXXIII

Of the Servant's Spiritual Daughter

'DAUGHTER, be of good comfort.'[1] At this time there lived a spiritual daughter of the Servant in a convent of the Order of Preachers at Töss.[2] She was called Elsbeth Stagel, and she led a very saintly life outwardly, and had an angelic mind inwardly. The noble ardour with which she devoted her heart and soul to God was such that all the vanities, through which many people lose their eternal salvation, fell away from her. All her diligence was bent on the pursuit of spiritual enlightenment, that she might be directed to a saintly and perfect life, for which she struggled with all her might.

She always wrote down everything beautiful that she came across that might foster in her and other persons divine virtues. In the convent, where she lived among the sisters as a mirror of all virtues, in spite of bodily sickness, she wrote a very good book. In this she related, among other things, the story of the saintly sisters now deceased, how blessed their lives were and what great miracles God wrought among them, which spurs on men of good will to devotion. This godly maiden became acquainted with the Servant of Eternal Wisdom, and she was drawn by God with great devotion to learn about his life and doctrine. By unobtrusive questioning she learnt the nature of his conversion and then she wrote it down, just as it is written above and below.

[1] Matthew, ix, 22; Luke, viii, 48.

[2] Near Winterthur, in Eastern Switzerland.

At the beginning of her life in religion, lofty and supernatural doctrines were imparted to her by a certain
teacher,[1] which were very sublime: of the naked Godhead, of the nothingness of all things, of the abandonment
of the self in the Nothing,[2] of the detachment of the
soul from all images, and many more such ideas, which
were clad in beautiful words and delightful to hear. But
in these things there lurked a certain secret danger for
simple and untrained persons. For the necessary distinc-
tions were entirely absent, so that the words might be
applied in one way or another, either to the body or the
mind, just as one thought fit.

Now this doctrine was good in itself, but it was not
suitable for her. She therefore wrote to the Servant,
asking him to help her and to guide her on the right way.
Nevertheless, she was still attracted by the doctrines she
had studied, and hence she suggested that he should
abandon crude teachings and write something about
these lofty doctrines.

In reply the Servant wrote: 'Good daughter, if thou
dost ask me about these high matters just from curiosity
in order to learn about them and to be proficient in dis-
cussing spiritual things, I can explain them to thee briefly
and in a few words. But thou shouldst not delight in them
overmuch, for in this way thou mayst easily stray into
pernicious error. True blessedness does not consist in fair
words, but in fair deeds. But if thou dost ask about these
things in order to carry them out in thy life, then put aside
the lofty questions and deal rather with those questions
that are fitting for thee. Thou seemest to be a young,
inexperienced nun, and it will therefore be more useful

[1] Meister Eckhart.

[2] The mystics often refer to God as Nothing, since He cannot be
defined.

[98]

for thee and those like thee to learn something of the first struggles of a beginner, of the life of self-discipline, and of good holy examples; how this or that Friend of God first applied himself to imitate the life and sufferings of Christ; what they suffered, as He did, and how they behaved, inwardly and outwardly, according as God drew them to Himself by sweetness or by severity, when and how images fell away from them. Look, by this means a beginner is encouraged and shown the right way, that he may go on to true holiness. Although God could give all this to man in one moment, He is not wont to do this; it must generally be won by effort and struggle.'

The daughter wrote to him again: 'I do not crave for wise words, but for a holy life. I have the courage to accomplish it fairly and honestly, however much it may hurt, whether it means sacrifice, or suffering, or death, or whatever it means; as long as it raises me up very near to God, it must be endured. And do not fear on account of the weakness of my constitution! All you dare bid me to do that causes pain to the physical nature I will dare to carry out, with the help of the divine strength. But first begin with the lowest things, and lead me along, just as one first teaches a young pupil what pertains to childhood, leading him on further and further, until he himself is master of all knowledge. I have only one more request of you: grant it to me for the sake of God, so that I shall not only be guided by you, but also strengthened in any adversity that may confront me.'

He asked her what her request was. She said: 'Sir, I have heard that the pelican is of such a nature that he bites himself and feeds his young in the nest with his own blood out of paternal love. Ah, sir, I mean that you should give yourself to me, your spiritual daughter, and feed me with the spiritual food of your good doctrine, and that you should not seek it far afield, but seek it near yourself. For the nearer it is to you, the more acceptable it will be to my longing soul.'

The Servant wrote again to her thus: 'Thou didst write to me recently about some sublime ideas that thou hadst selected from the sweet doctrine of the saintly Meister Eckhart, which thou, as was fitting, didst treat so tenderly. I wonder greatly that after such a noble draught of the sublime master, thou shouldst thirst for the coarse drink of the humble servant. But if I see it aright, I recognize with joy thy good sense in this matter, in that thou dost ply me so actively with questions as to the beginning of a noble and well-directed life, and the preliminary exercises by which a person can attain thereto.'

CHAPTER XXXIV

Of the First Steps of a Beginner

'THE beginning of a holy life, daughter, is of various kinds: one person begins in one way, another in another. But I will gladly tell thee of the beginning of which thou dost enquire. I know a man in Christ[1] who, when he began, first cleared his conscience by a general confession. All his diligence was directed towards making a good confession, by laying bare his sins before a wise confessor, in order to leave the confessor, who stands in the place of God, clean and pure, after forgiveness of his sins, as happened to Mary Magdalene, when with a penitent heart and weeping eyes, she washed His divine feet, and God forgave her all her sins.[2] That was the first step of this man on the way to God.'

[1] That is, Suso himself.   [2] Luke, vii, 37–8, 48.

The daughter took this example very much to heart, and wanted to follow it immediately, and it occurred to her in her eagerness that the Servant was the best person to whom to confess. She also thought that by this confession she would become his daughter in religion, and would be more fully entrusted to his care in pious loyalty.

Now, as it happened, the confession could not be made orally. So she thought over her whole life, which was in truth pure and clean, and wrote down all the sins of which in her opinion, she had ever been guilty, on a large wax tablet. She sent to him the sealed tablet, and asked him to absolve her from her sins. When he had read the tablet to the end, he saw at the foot the words: 'Gracious sir, I now fall before your feet, sinful woman that I am, and beg you with your faithful heart to take me to the heart of God, and that I may be called your child in time and in eternity.'

He was deeply touched by this confiding devotion of his daughter, and turning to God he said: 'Merciful Lord, what should I, Thy servant, say to this? Should I reject her? Lord, I could not do that to a little dog. Lord, if I did that, perchance it would displease Thee. She seeks the wealth of the lord in the servant. Ah, gentle Lord of mine, I fall at Thy sacred feet, and pray Thee, merciful Lord, to hear her prayer. May she be rewarded for her faith and for her sincere confidence, for she is crying out after us. What didst Thou do for the heathen woman?[1] Ah, merciful heart, lo, we hear such hearty praise of Thy boundless mercy to us, and even if her sins were much greater, Thou wouldst forgive her. Ah, gentle heart, turn Thy merciful eyes to her and say to her: "Daughter, be of good comfort, thy faith hath made thee whole,"[2] and

[1] Matthew, xv, 22-8.

[2] Matthew, ix, 22; Luke, viii, 48.

confirm it in my stead, for I have done my part and wished her full absolution for all her sins.'

He wrote back to her by the same messenger: 'What thou hast asked of God through the Servant, has been granted. Know also that God had shown him all this beforehand. This very morning he was sitting after his prayers for a quiet rest, when many divine mysteries were revealed to him. For some time he had heavenly converse with angelic spirits, and his soul was glad with this over-flowing miracle that had been vouchsafed to him. Then it seemed to him in his vision that thou didst come to Him in the place where He sat among the heavenly host. Thou didst kneel before Him with great earnestness and bow down thy face towards His heart, kneeling thus with thy head resting for some time on His Heart, and in the sight of the angels who stood by. The friar was amazed at thy boldness, and yet so holy was thy manner that He graciously permitted it. Thou knowest full well what favour was vouchsafed to thee by the heavenly Father, and it could be seen in thy face, for when thou didst rise up, after a long while, thy face was shining so full of grace that it could well be seen that God had conferred on thee some special gift, and will continue to do so by that same heart, that God may be glorified thereby, and that thou mayst be comforted.

Something similar befell also a godly woman who was a noble maiden in a castle. Her name was Anna and all her life she was continually in pain. Through her God wrought great miracles, from her youth until her death. Before she had become acquainted with the Servant, or had even heard of him, she was once in an ecstasy in her devotions, and she saw the saints in the heavenly courts seeing and praising God. Then she asked her dear lord and apostle St. John, to whom she had a special devotion, to hear her confession. Then he said very kindly to her:

'I will give thee a good confessor in my stead, to whom God has given entire power over thee. He can console thee well in thy manifold sufferings.' She asked him who it was and where, and what his name was. All this was revealed to her. She thanked God, and set out on her way early in the morning, and went to the friary, to which she had been directed by God, and enquired about him. He came to her to the gate and asked what her business was. She began, and told him, and confessed to him; and hearing the divine message, he carried it out and took charge of her.

This holy daughter told him that she had once seen in the spirit a beautiful rose tree well adorned with red roses, and on the rose tree appeared the child *Jesus* with a chaplet of red roses. Under the rose tree she saw the Servant sitting. The child plucked many roses and then threw them on the Servant, so that he was entirely strewn with red roses. She asked the child what the roses signified, and he said: 'The number of the roses is the manifold sufferings that God will send him, which he should accept kindly from God and endure patiently.'

CHAPTER XXXV

Of the First Examples and Teachings for a Beginner,
and the Need for Moderation in Austerities

WHEN the Servant, in his beginning, had been sufficiently purified by confession, he drew in his thoughts three circles round himself, behind which he kept himself enclosed in spiritual care. The first circle was his cell, his chapel and the choir: when he was in this circle he felt quite safe. The second was the whole friary, except the gate. The third and outermost was the gate, and even there he had to be on his guard. When he left these three circles, he felt like a wild animal that has left its lair and is pursued by the hunt. He then required wisdom and watchfulness.

At the beginning, he chose out as his secret place of refuge a chapel, where he could do his devotions in artistic surroundings. In particular, there was a painting on parchment of Eternal Wisdom, which he had made in his youth. She has heaven and earth in her power, and in her fair loveliness she surpasses all earthly creatures in beauty, for which reason he had chosen her as his love in the flower of his youth. He carried this lovely picture with him when he went to school,[1] put it in the window of his cell, and looked at it with eyes full of love and deep longing. He brought it back home again with him, and hung it in the chapel for loving memory. The other pictures and images that were there, which related to the spiritual life, as it pertains to him and other beginners, may be illustrated by the paintings and sayings from the ancient Fathers.

Some of these sayings follow below, as they are depicted in the chapel.

St. Arsenius asked the angel what he should do to be saved, and the angel said: 'Thou shalt flee, be silent, and sink into peace.' Afterwards, in a vision the angel read to the Servant out of the *Book of the Ancient Fathers:*[2] 'The source of all blessedness is stillness and unity within thee.'

Theodorus: To keep oneself pure produces more learning than hard study.

Abbot Moyses: Sit in thy cell, and thou shalt learn all things.

[1] At Cologne.

[2] *Vitae Patrum,* in Migne, *Patrologia Latina,* Vols. 73–4.

Abbot Johannes: A fish out of water is like a monk out of his cloister.

Antonius: The mortification of the flesh and devotion of the soul and flight from men can bring forth chastity— Thou shalt wear no garment in which vanity may be seen. — The first fight of a beginner is to set himself firmly against gluttony.

Pastor: Thou shalt not be angry with any man until he wants to put out thy right eye.

Isidorus: An angry man displeases God, however great the signs he works.

Ipericius: It is a lesser sin to eat meat, if it is avoidable, than to slander thy neighbour behind his back.

Pyor: It is very evil to expose the failings of others, and to conceal one's own.

Zacharias: A man must bear great disgrace if he is ever to establish his own salvation.

Nestor: Thou must first be an ass, before thou canst possess divine wisdom.

Senex: Thou shalt stand immovable in joy and sorrow like the bones of the dead.

Helias: A pale complexion, an emaciated body, and humble conduct well befit a religious.

Hilarion: One should cut off the food off a horse that is too lustful, or of a body that is unchaste.

Senex: A Father said: 'Put away the wine from me, for the death of the soul is hidden within it.'

Pastor: He never became a spiritual man who goes on complaining, and who cannot refrain from anger, impatience and loquacity.

Cassian: As the dying Christ on the cross Himself, our conduct should be formed on His model.

Antonius said to a monk: 'Brother, help thyself, otherwise neither I nor God will ever help thee.'

Arsenius: A woman begged a Father to remember her

in his prayers. He said: 'I pray God to destroy thy image in my heart.'

Macarius: I inflict many hardships on my body, because I have many temptations from it.

Johannes: A Father of the Church, said: 'I never had my own way, and never taught in words what I did not do myself in deeds.'

Senex: Many fair words without works are like the luxuriant tree that bears foliage without much fruit.

Nilus: He who must walk much in this world must also receive many wounds.

Senex: If thou canst do naught else, stay in thy cell for the sake of God.

Ipericius: He who guards his chastity is honoured here, and crowned by God hereafter.

Appollonius: Beware of beginnings, and defend thy head against the serpent.

Agathon: A Father said: 'I have carried a stone in my mouth for three years, in order to learn how to be silent.'

St. Syncletices: If thou art sick to death, be glad, for God has remembered thee. If thou art ill, do not cast the blame on thy fasting, for they who do not fast are ill likewise. If thou art tried by the temptations of the flesh, rejoice, for thou mayst become a second Paul.

Nestorius: A good monk said: 'The sun never shone on me while I was eating.'

Johannes: A second one said: 'Nor on me in anger.'

Paphnucius: It is of no use to begin, unless one brings it to a good end.

Abbot Moyses: Whatever deprives thee of a pure mind must be avoided, however good it seems.

Cassian: All perfection is achieved when the soul, with all its powers, is absorbed into the only One, who is God.

The Servant sent these maxims and precepts of the Fathers to his daughter in religion, and she took it to heart, and thought it meant that she should exercise her body with great austerities, according to the strict example of the Fathers. So she began to mortify the flesh, and to torment herself grievously with hair shirts, with thongs and dreadful chains, with sharp iron nails, and many such things.

When the Servant became aware of this, he sent her this message: 'Dear daughter, if thou dost desire to direct thy spiritual life according to my doctrine, as thou hast asked of me, give up this excessive austerity, for it is not fitting for thy woman's weakness and thy health. Our dear Lord did not say: "Take *My* cross upon you," but "Let every man take *his* cross upon him." Thou shalt not endeavour to imitate the mortifications of the Fathers, or the hard austerities of thy spiritual father. Thou shouldst select out of all these only a part, as much as thou canst carry out with thy weak body, in order that sin may die out within thee and that thou mayst live long in the body. That is an ardous task and the best for thee.'

She now wished to know from him why he himself imposed such strict austerities on himself, but he would not advise her or any other persons to do likewise. Then he referred her to the Holy Scriptures and said: 'It is written, that once among the Fathers many led such an inhuman and incredibly strict life that in these latter days it is an abomination to some soft natures even to hear of them. They never realized what devout zeal is capable of performing, and what it can do with divine strength, and suffer for the sake of God. It is possible for such a devout man to accomplish the impossible in God, just as David said that with God's help he would break through a strong wall.[1] Yet it is also written in the *Lives*

[1] Psalm, xviii, 29 (A.V.). Suso follows the text of the Vulgate, Psalm, xvii, 30.

of the Ancient Fathers, that some of them did not impose on themselves such great mortifications, and nevertheless they endeavoured to reach the same goal as the others. St. Peter and St. John were drawn to God by different paths.

'Who can explain these wonders, save the Lord, Who is wonderful in His Friends,[1] and wishes to be praised in manifold ways? To this end, moreover, we are of different natures: what is suitable for one is not fitting for another. Hence, if perchance one man has not practised austerities, one should not conclude that he is so beset with obstacles that he cannot attain to the highest. On the other hand, soft natures should not despise and judge maliciously such severe austerities in others. Let every one give heed only to himself, and heed what God wants of him. Let him accomplish this and leave other things alone.

'In general, it is much better to practise moderate severity than immoderate. But as the middle way is toilsome to find, it is more advisable to stop a little short of it than to venture too far beyond it. For if one does immoderate violence to nature, it often happens that one must yield immoderately to her later; although it is true that many a great saint has overlooked this in his excess of zeal. This strict life, and the examples of which we have spoken, may be useful to those who pamper themselves too much, and slacken the bridle of their rebellious natures too wantonly and to their eternal loss, but this does not apply to thee and those like thee. God has many kinds of crosses, with which He chastises His Friends. I foresee that God will lay another cross upon thy back, which will hurt thee more than such chastisement. Bear this cross patiently, when it comes upon thee!'

Not long after, God visited the spiritual daughter

[1] From the Vulgate, Psalm, lxvii, 36 (this verse is not in the Authorized Version, Psalm, lxviii).

with a chronic illness, so that she remained until death a poor sick creature in the body. She sent him a message to say that it had come to pass as he had predicted. Then he wrote to her again: 'God has not only struck thee. He has also wounded me in wounding thee, for I have no one else who could help me with industry and pious devotion to finish my little book, as thou didst, when thou wert well. Therefore the Servant prays earnestly to God for Thee, that if it be His will, He may give thee thy health again.' Now God did not answer his prayer at once, so he was angry with God in a friendly manner, and he thought he would not write any more little books about the God he loved. He also intended to give up his accustomed morning greeting from annoyance, unless God made her well again.

'As he sat down, as was his custom, in his chapel, restless at heart, he fell into an ecstasy, and it seemed to him as if an angel host came into the chapel before him. They sang a heavenly song to comfort him, for they knew that at this particular hour he was particularly sorrowful. They asked him why he was so sad, and did not join in with them in song. Then he confessed to them the disorderly aberration of which he had been guilty before Almighty God, because He had not hearkened to his prayer for thy health. Then they remarked that he should refrain from this, for God had ordained the sickness for thee for the best of reasons. It was to be thy cross in this world, by which means thou shouldst acquire much merit here, and manifold reward in heaven. Therefore, be patient, my daughter and just accept it as a kind gift from God the beloved.'

CHAPTER XXXVI

Of the Childlike Devotion of a Beginner in Religion

ONCE, when the Servant had come to the convent, and wanted to see his sick daughter, she asked him to relate something of divine matters, which did not fill the soul with deep earnestness, but yet were pleasant for a godly soul to hear. He then told her of his childlike devotion, saying: 'When the Servant was in the flower of his youth it was his long continued custom, when he was bled by the surgeon, to go at once to his beloved God on the cross. There he raised up his wounded arm, and said with a deep sigh: "Ah, Friend of my heart, remember that it is the custom for a man to go to his beloved when he has been bled, for some good blood. Now Thou knowest, dear Lord, that I have no other beloved than Thee. Therefore, I come to thee, so that Thou mayest bless my wound and make good blood for me." '

Also, when he put on a new coat, or a new cape, he generally went first to his accustomed place, and begged his heavenly Lord, who had provided him with the garment, to wish him happiness and health therein, and to help him always to wear it according to His will,

Earlier, in his childhood, he had the following custom: when the beautiful spring came, and the gentle flowers first began to bloom, he restrained himself, and would not pluck any flowers until he had first remembered his spiritual beloved, the gentle flower and maiden of roses, the Mother of God, with his first flowers. When the right time seemed to have come, he plucked the flowers with many loving thoughts, carried them into his cell, and made a lovely chaplet out of them. He went with it into the choir, or into the Lady Chapel, knelt down humbly before the image of Our Lady, placing the lovely wreath of flowers on her image. Since she was the most beautiful flower of all and the summer delight of his heart, he thought that she would not despise the first flowers of her servant.

Once, when he had thus crowned the fair one, it seemed to him in a vision that the sky was open, and he saw the bright angels going up and down in heavenly garments. Then he heard the most beautiful song that was ever heard, sung by the cheerful host in the heavenly courts. In particular, they sang a song to Our Lady, that sounded so passing sweet that his soul melted away in great bliss. It was like the hymn sung on All Saints' Day in the sequence *Illic regina virginum, transcendens culmen ordinum;* and the sense of the hymn is that the pure Queen soars above all the heavenly host, in honour and glory. He struck up and sang with the heavenly host. Much of the heavenly savour and longing for God remained afterwards in his soul.

On another Mayday, later, he had, as was his wont, placed with great devotion a little garland of roses on his dearest heavenly Lady. Early the same morning, as he had come from afar and was tired, he wanted to have a little sleep, and did not salute the Virgin at the accustomed hour. Now when the usual time for getting up arrived, and he should have risen, he felt as if he was in the midst of a heavenly choir, which was singing the *Magnificat,* in praise of the Mother of God. When this was over, the Virgin came forward and ordered the friar to sing the verse *O vernalis rosa,* which means 'O thou fair rose of summer.' He wondered what she meant, and yet wished to be obedient to her, so he began to sing with a joyous heart 'O vernalis rosa'. And at once three or four youths of the heavenly host, who were standing in the choir, joined in too, and then the other group did likewise, all singing together in unison. They sang so soulfully, and it sounded as if all the instruments in the world were joining in. His mortal nature could no longer endure this excess of melody, and he came to himself.

On the day after Our Lady's Day, the Assumption,[1] great joy was once more shown him in the heavenly courts. They would not admit anyone who was unworthy. The Servant would gladly have entered, but a youth came, seizing him by the hand, and saying: 'Fellow, this time thou hast no right to go in, stay here outside. Thou art in disgrace, and must be punished for thy misdeeds before thou mayst hear the heavenly song.' And he led him down a crooked path into a hole in the ground, that was dark and gloomy. He could not walk backwards or forwards, but was like a man who is in prison and who cannot see the sun or the moon. This made him sorrowful and he began to sigh and to complain because of his imprisonment.

Soon after the youth came to him and asked him how he was. He said: 'Very bad.' Then the youth said: 'Know that the Queen of heaven is angered with thee because of the transgression for which thou art imprisoned here.' The Servant was sore afraid and said: 'Woe is me, wretch that I am! What have I done against her?' He said: 'She is angry with thee because thou art unwilling to preach of her on her festivals, and yesterday at her great festival, thou didst refuse to accede to thy superior's bidding to preach of her.' He said: 'Alas, my friend and lord, methinks she is worthy of such high honour that I feel too small, and commend it rather to those who can preach more worthily than a poor man like me.'

Then said the youth: 'Know then, that she likes thee to do it, and it is an acceptable service to her. Therefore, do not do it again.' The Servant began to weep, and said

[1] 15th August.

[*112*]

to the youth: 'Ah, dear youth, reconcile me with the pure Mother, for I pledge my faith that it will not occur again.' The youth smiled and comforted him kindly, and took him out of the prison and back home again, saying: 'I have noticed from the kind look and words of the Queen of heaven towards thee that her anger against thee has abated. She will always show her maternal love to thee.'

It was his custom, when he left or entered his cell, to make his way through the choir past the reserved sacrament, and he thought to himself: He who has a dear friend anywhere on his road will gladly lengthen his way a little for the sake of a little friendly conversation.

A man[1] once asked God for a Carnival gift, since he did not wish to have one from any creature. And in an ecstasy, he seemed to see the dear Christ coming in the form He had when He was thirty years old, and he thought He was coming to fulfil his desire and to give him a heavenly Carnival. He took a chalice full of wine in His hand, and offered it to three men who were sitting there at table, to each in turn. The first sank down powerless, the second was also rather weak, but the third did not heed Him. Then the Lord told him the difference between a beginner, a progressing man and a perfect man, and explained how differently they behaved in the presence of divine sweetness.

With these and similar divine conversations, the tale of the Servant came to a close. She wrote everything down secretly and put it in a locked chest, there to be preserved and concealed. Once a good sister came to the woman who had kept it, and said to her: 'Ah, dear sister, what hidden divine wonders hast thou in thy chest? Look, last night in a dream I thought a joyful heavenly boy was standing in thy chest. He held in his hand a sweet instrument that they call a two-stringed fiddle, and thereon he

[1] Suso.

played spiritual dances that were so charming that everyone drank spiritual joy and pleasure from them. I pray
of thee, take out what thou hast kept locked up, so that
we also may read it.' She was silent and would not tell
her aught of it, for she had been forbidden to speak
about it.

CHAPTER XXXVII

How He drew Dissolute Persons to God, and comforted the Suffering

ONCE the Servant had not sent any news to his daughter
in religion for a long time. So she wrote him a letter, in
which she said that she wanted to have a letter from him,
by means of which her sorrowing heart might be lifted
up once more. Then he wrote: 'In order that thou mayst
be the more patient in thy sufferings, I will tell thee something of pain, to the glory of God. I knew a man whom
God had ordained to be so afflicted that he had to witness
the public destruction of his good name in the world.
The desire of this man was filled with the thought of
loving God from the depths of his soul, to commend
heartily to all men the same adorable beloved and to draw
them away from all other frivolous loves. When he had
thus plucked away from the devil his own and brought
them back to God, the Evil One was much displeased,
and he appeared to some good persons, threatening that
he would avenge himself on the Servant.'

Once the Servant visited a monastery of an order in
which the monks are wont to live in one lodging and
the nuns of the order in another building.[1] In this monas-

[1] The Benedictines and Augustinian Canons had double monasteries of this kind.

tery there were two religious, a man and a woman, who were attached to each other, and in bondage to great love and dangerous intimacy. The devil had hidden the truth from them in their blind hearts, so that they regarded their sin as if it was no sin or wickedness, but was permitted by God. When the Servant was asked in confidence if this could really continue according to God's will, he said: 'No, by no means.' And he told them that the light was false and contrary to Christian teaching, and he saw to it that they gave it up and kept themselves pure thereafter.

While he thus acted, there was a holy woman called Anna, who was at her devotions. She was in an ecstasy, and saw in the spirit a large host of devilish spirits, gathering above the Servant in the air, and all crying together: 'Death, death to the bad friar!' They upbraided and cursed him, because he had driven them from this pleasant place by his counsel, and all swore together with terrifying gestures that they would plot against him, until they had had their revenge upon him. But as they could neither attack him in his body nor in his possessions, they wanted to vilify him in the integrity of his reputation before men in a horrible manner. They intended to cast dishonourable suspicions on him, and however much he tried to avoid giving them occasion for it, they were determined to bring it about by low cunning. At this the saintly nun Anna was sore afraid, and she prayed to Our dear Lady to come to his help in his coming trials. Then the mild Mother said to her kindly: 'They can do nothing to him save with the permission of my Son; what he ordains for him is and will remain the most salutary and best for him. So bid him be of good courage.'

When she had told the friar of this, he began to be very afraid of the hostile gathering of evil spirits, and went, as he was accustomed to do in his trials, up the hill where there is a chapel, dedicated in honour of the holy angels. As was his custom, he went there nine times round the chapel, praying in honour of the nine choirs of angels, and he earnestly begged them to be his helpers against all his foes. Early in the morning, he was led in the spirit to a beautiful field. There he saw around him a very large host of angelic youths, who wished to help him. They comforted him and spake thus: 'God is with thee, and will never desert thee in thy need. Therefore, do not cease to draw wordly hearts to divine love!' He was strengthened thereby, and earnestly strove to bring back wild and tame creatures to God.

He had won over with kind words a lawless man, who had gone for eighteen years without ever confessing his sins. He gained confidence in the Servant with God's help, and confessed to him so remorsefully that they both wept. The sinner died shortly afterwards, and had a blessed end.

Once he converted twelve fallen women from their sinful life. What he suffered through them cannot be told. At the end, only two of them remained steadfast.

There were, moreover, here and there in the country, a number of women, secular and religious, who through the weakness of their character had openly fallen into sinful habits. These poor girls had no one to whom they dared in their shame confess their bitter grief of heart, so that from fear and distress they often fell into the temptation to kill themselves. But when they heard that the Servant had a forgiving heart for all sufferers, they made bold to come to him, each at the time of her greatest need, and they confided in him all the fears and distress to which they were in bondage. When he saw these poor creatures suffering so wretchedly, he wept with them and comforted them kindly. He helped them, and often staked his reputation in order to rehabilitate them in soul

[*116*]

and in repute, letting evil tongues wag as much as they chose.

Among others there was one of high birth, who felt great remorse for her fall. Our Lady appeared to her and said: 'Go to my chaplain; he will help thee.' She said: 'Alas, Lady, I do not know him.' The Mother of Mercy said: 'See, here under my cloak I have him under my protection; look well at his face that thou mayst know him. He is a helper in need and a comforter of all suffering persons. He will console thee.' She came to him from a foreign land, and recognized his face, as she had seen him before in the spirit. She begged him to reconcile her with God, and told him what had happened. And he received her gently, and helped her to the best of his powers, as the Mother of Mercy had bidden him.

CHAPTER XXXVIII

Of a Sore Affliction that befell Him about this Time

ONE evening he put up at an inn, and when the morning was approaching, he was led in a vision to a place where Mass was about to be sung. He himself was to sing it, the lot having fallen upon him. The choristers began the Mass of the martyrs: *Multae tribulationes justorum,* which tells of the many tribulations of the Friends of God. He was displeased to hear it, and would gladly have changed it, so he said: 'Ah, why do you din all this about martyrs into our ears? Why are you singing about martyrs, seeing that it is not a martyr's day that we are celebrating?' Then they looked at him and pointed at him, and said: 'God will find his martyrs to-day, as He has always found them. Make thyself ready and sing for thyself!'

[*117*]

Then he turned over the pages of the missal that was in front of him, and he would fain have sung the Mass of a confessor or anything else, rather than that of the martyrs, but whatever page he turned to, everything was full of martyrs. Seeing, however, that there was no help for it, he sang with them, and his song sounded very sad. After a short time he said: 'This is strange; one would rather sing *Gaudeamus* joyfully, than sing of sad things like the martyrs.' They said: 'Good fellow, thou dost know nothing! This sad hymn of martyrs comes first, and them later, when it is time, comes the cheerful hymn *Gaudeamus*.'

When he awoke, his heart trembled because of this vision, and he said : 'Alas, God, must I again suffer martyrdom?' So he went on his way with a sad countenance, and his companion said to him: 'Ah, father, what ails you? Why do you bear yourself so sorrowfully?' He answered: 'Alas, dear friend, I must sing the Mass of martyrs here,' meaning that God had revealed to him that he must suffer like a martyr. But his companion could not understand him; so he was silent, and kept his thoughts to himself.

When he reached the town, the dark days before Christmas had begun. Then it was that his bitter trials began, as so often before, but this time they were so severe that, as the phrase goes, he felt as if his heart would break, if this has ever happened to a suffering man. Now this was the nature of his bitter sorrow: among other persons whom he would gladly have brought back to God, there was a deceitful, treacherous woman. She had the heart of a wolf, and concealed it so carefully beneath a decent exterior, that for a long time the friar did not notice anything wrong. She had formerly led a very sinful and unchaste life with a man, and increased her guilt by ascribing the paternity of her child to another man, who declared himself to be entirely innocent in the matter.

The Servant did not turn away the girl because of her misdoings, but heard her confession; and she helped him more than others did in needful and honourable service after the custom of those priests who are called 'Terminarii.'[1]

This had been going on for some time quite satisfactorily, when he, and other honourable men, clearly observed that once again she had secretly fallen into her evil ways. He said nothing of it, not wishing to betray her, but he broke with her and put an end to her services. When she became aware of this, she sent him word that he was not to do this. If he deprived her of her earnings, he would pay for it, for she would father a child on him that she had had by a wealthy man. He would have to be the father of the child, and she would give him such a bad name with the child that he would be everywhere in disrepute.

When he heard these words, he was afraid and quite taken aback. He groaned and said to himself: 'Fear and trouble compass me around, and I do not know whither I should turn. If I do it, woe to me, and if I do not, woe again! And in this way I am environed by grief and distress on all hands, and I might well perish as a result.' So he waited with a heart full of alarm, to see what God had permitted the devil to inflict on him. He took counsel with God and with himself, and came to the conclusion that of the two sad alternatives the best thing for his body and his soul was to break with the wicked woman, however much his reputation might suffer thereby. And he did so.

She was then so enraged with him in her cruel heart that she ran round to clergy and laity, and in her devilish malice she slandered herself scandalously, merely in order

[1] Mendicant friars to whom a fixed district was allotted for collecting alms.

to bring trouble on the poor man. She told everyone she had conceived a child, and that the friar was the father. This caused great scandal among all who believed her words, and the scandal was all the greater because the fame of his sanctity was so widespread.

All this pierced his heart and soul to the quick, and he went about, absorbed in his own sad thoughts, beset by woe and grief. He had long days and bitter nights, and even his brief rest was broken by anguish. He looked up to God reproachfully, and said with deep sighs: 'Alas, God, the hour of my grief has come! How should I, how can I endure this misery and sorrow of my heart? O God, would that I were dead, if only I could no longer see or hear such sorrowful tidings! Lord, Lord, I have now honoured Thy worthy name all my days and proclaimed it far and wide, and taught many a man to love and honour it. Wilt thou now thus plunge my name into dishonour? This is my great complaint, that the worthy Order of Preachers must now come into disrepute through me. That is to-day and evermore my complaint! Alas, for the woe of my heart! All those pure persons who respected me before as a saintly man—which often gave me new courage—woe is me, they now regard me as an evil and worldly deceiver, whereby my heart and soul are wounded and pierced.'

When the poor sufferer had fretted about this for some time, and his body and frame were wasting away with grief, a woman came to him and said: 'Ah, good sir, why do you run so lamentably to your destruction? I will give you counsel and help, and if you will obey me, no harm will come to your reputation. Have courage!' He looked up and said: 'Alas, how wilt thou bring this about?' She said: 'I will secretly take the child under my cloak, and bury it alive at night or drive a needle into its brain, so that it will die. If once the child is under the

[*120*]

earth, the evil gossip will also be buried, and you shall preserve your honour.' He said with a furious voice; 'Alas, thou wicked murderess with thy murderous heart! Wilt thou slay the innocent babe? What fault is it of the child that its mother is an evil woman? Wilt thou bury it alive? No, no, God forbid that this murder should ever take place on my account! See, the worst that can occur to me through this matter is the loss of my reputation; but even if the honour of a whole country depended on me, I would gladly entrust it to Almighty God, rather than allow the innocent babe to perish.'

She said: 'Well, is it not your child after all? What does it matter to you?' And she drew forth a sharp pointed knife and said: 'Just let me take the child away from your sight, and I will cut its throat, or thrust this knife into its heart; then it will be dead on the spot, and you will have peace.' He answered: 'Be silent, unclean, evil devil! No matter to whom it may belong on this earth, it is made in God's image and redeemed at the price of bitter pain by the precious and innocent blood of Christ. Hence I will not permit its young innocent blood to be shed.'

She said impatiently: 'If you will not have it killed, let it be carried secretly, early in the morning, into the church, and it will be treated like other foundlings. Otherwise you will have great expense and great trials till the boy is grown up.' He answered: 'I put my trust in the great God of heaven; hitherto He has nourished me in my loneliness, and He will doubtless also be able to provide for us both.'

And he said to her: 'Go and bring me the child in secret that I may see it!' He put the child on his knee, and looked at it, and it smiled at him. Then he sighed from the depths of his heart and said: 'Am I to kill this smiling pretty child? Indeed not. I will rather suffer any calamity that may fall upon me.' And he turned gently to the babe and said these words: 'Alas, thou poor forsaken child, what a sad orphan thou art! For thy own faithless father has denied thee; thy murderous mother wanted to cast thee away like a troublesome spurned dog. Now God's decree has given thee to me, so that I needs must be thy father: and that I will be gladly. I will accept thee from God and from no one else. Ah, child of my heart! Thou dost sit now on my sad lap, and dost look at me kindly, and yet thou canst not speak. Ah, I look at thee with a wounded heart; with the tears of my eyes and the kisses of my lips I pour upon thy childlike face the flood of my hot tears.'

When the pretty little boy felt the big tears of the weeping man running so fast over his little eyes, he began to cry bitterly, and thus they both wept together. And, seeing the child thus weeping, he pressed it lovingly to his heart and said: 'Hush, my precious one! Ah, dearest child, am I to kill thee, because thou art not my child, and because I must toil hard to support thee? Ah, fair, dear one, my gentle child, look, I cannot indeed do thee any harm save to claim thee as my child and God's. As long as God grants me as much as a single mouthful of food, I will share it with thee, to the praise of God, Who is my beloved, and I will patiently bear everything that I may be called upon to bear, my gentle child.'

When the cruel-hearted woman, who had previously wanted to kill the child, saw and heard the tears and caresses, she was touched to the heart with such great pity that she broke into weeping and crying, and he had to comfort her, fearing that someone might come and see them. At last, when she had wept her fill, he handed back the child to her, blessed it and said: 'Now, may the dear God bless thee, may the holy angels protect thee from all harm!' And he had it provided with all it needed at his expense.

Then the wicked woman, the mother of the child, set to work with redoubled efforts, and if she had hitherto vilified him badly enough, she now did so much more, and injured him in every possible way. Consequently, many pure and virtuous souls had compassion on him, and they often wished that God, the righteous One, might take her away from the world.

It once chanced that one of his friends in the world came to him and said: 'Alas, sir, it is a great crime that this woman has committed against you. By God, I will inflict stern retribution on her. I will stand unobserved on the long bridge that spans the river.¹ And when she crosses it, I will push the blasphemer over and drown her, so that this foul crime of hers may be avenged.'

He said: 'No, friend, God forbid, that a living human being should be slain for my sake. God, who knows all hidden things, knows that she has wronged me with regard to the child. I entrust the matter to His hands. Let Him slay her at once, or let her live, as is His will. And I say to thee: even if I wanted to jeopardize my own salvation, by bringing about her death, yet I would wish to honour in her the name of all pure women, and I would wish her to live.'

The man said very angrily: 'I would as soon kill such a woman as a man, if she had denounced me so villainously.' He replied: 'No, that would be senseless cruelty, and immoral savagery. Refrain from this, and let justice be done, let all the grief fall upon me that God wishes me to suffer.'

His troubles increased more and more, his suffering heart was overwhelmed, and he yearned for a little help and consolation in his distress. So he went out and sought for comfort, especially at the hands of two friends, who

¹ Probably the Rhine at Constance.

as long as he had been at the summit of the wheel of fortune, had behaved as if they were his faithful friends and brothers. He wished to seek from them some solace for his suffering heart. Alas, then God showed him by the behaviour of these two that there is no dependence on creatures, for he was openly snubbed by them, more than he ever was by the common people. One of the two friends received the suffering friar very harshly, and turned away his face angrily, behaving very contemptuously, with sneering words. Among the other deeply insulting remarks he made, he said most haughtily: 'I will have nothing more to do with you. Not only your sermons, but also the books you have written should be condemned.' He answered very gently, looked up to the heavens, and said: 'I put my trust in Almighty God. May He grant that my books may be more valued and loved than ever before, when the time comes.'

In this town his necessities had been provided for by some kind-hearted persons. But as he was slandered by these false rumours, his well-wishers believed the calumnies against him, and withdrew their help and friendship from him, until they were admonished and enlightened by divine truth to return to him.

Once, as he sat down to take a quiet rest, he fell into a trance, and it seemed as if he were being transported into a supernatural region. Then something spoke to him in the depths of his soul, thus: 'Listen, listen to a word of consolation that I shall read to thee.' He stretched forward and listened intently. Then the voice began and read in Latin the chapter from none[1] set for Christmas Eve: 'Non vocaberis ultra derelicta.' This means: 'Henceforth thou shalt not be called "the forsaken of God", and thy land shall not be called the "devastated earth". Thou shalt be called "The will of God is in thee", and thy land

[1] A devotional service sung at the ninth hour (3 p.m.).

shall be cultivated, for the heavenly Father has pleasure in thee.'[1]

When these words had been read to the end, the voice began to read them again, four times over. He said, in amazement: 'Beloved, what does it signify that thou shouldst say these words so often to me?' The answer came: 'I do it to strengthen thee in thy trust in God, Who will provide for the land of His friends, that is, for their mortal body, according to their need. And if in one respect they are lacking, He will add in another all that they require. Thus will God deal with thee as a father does.'

On one occasion in particular, when he was sorrowful because of his sufferings, a voice spoke thus within him: 'Remember that Christ did not want to have only His beloved disciple John and the loyal St. Peter in His society. He was also willing to suffer the wicked Judas to be with him. Thou dost desire to be a follower of Christ, and will not suffer thy Judas willingly.' Swiftly an answer flashed into his mind: 'Ah, Lord, if a suffering Friend of God had only one Judas, it would be bearable, but at present every corner is full of Judases, and when one goes away, four or five others come forth.' An answering thought flashed at once into his mind: 'To a man who is righteous, no Judas should be thought of as a Judas. He should be regarded as a co-worker with God, through whom he is to be tried as may be best for his own good. When Judas betrayed Christ with a kiss, Christ called him His friend, saying, "My friend." '[2]

This poor man had suffered thus for some time in great wretchedness, but he clung nevertheless to one small consolation, namely, that his crushing burden had not yet come to the knowledge of the judges and authorities of his Order. Yet God snatched away from him even this

[1] Isaiah, lxii, 4.   [2] Matthew, xxvi, 50.

[125]

grain of comfort, for the General of the whole Order and the Provincial of the Province of Germany came together to the city in which the worthy man had been slandered by the wicked woman. When the poor man, who was at that time living elsewhere,[1] heard this piece of news, his heart fainted within him, and he thought: 'As soon as the authorities hear this wicked woman's words against thee, thou art as good as dead. They will impose such heavy penance on thee that a physical death would be preferable.' This painful distress lasted for twelve consecutive days and nights, during which he awaited the terrible punishment they would inflict upon him.

Once, when he was sitting in an ecstasy, it seemed to him in a vision that one of his spiritual daughters came up to him. While she lived, she had often said that he must suffer very much, but that God would release him. She appeared to him now, and comforted him kindly. But he took it in bad part, and denied that she was speaking the truth. She smiled and stepped towards him, gave him her saintly hand, and said: 'Accept my word as a Christian, in the name of Almighty God, that God will not desert you. He will help you to overcome this and all your afflictions.' He said: 'See, daughter, my sufferings are so great that I cannot believe thee, unless thou givest me a sign.' She said: 'God Himself will exculpate you in all good, pure hearts. Things appear to evil hearts in accordance with their own wickedness, but a wise Friend of God takes no heed thereof. The Order of Preachers, which you accuse, will be all the more acceptable to God and all prudent men on your account. Let this be a sign to you: Lo, God will soon avenge you, and will strike with His wrathful hand the wicked-hearted woman who has thus afflicted you. He will cut her life short, and all those who have particularly aided her in

[1] Probably at Ulm.

her slanders must be punished soon; be certain of this.' The friar was greatly comforted thereby, and waited confidently until God saw fit to end the matter.

Shortly afterwards it all actually came to pass, just as she had predicted. The monster of iniquity who had so tortured him died a sudden death. A number of others, who had been among his worst tormentors, were snatched away hence by death. Some of them died unconscious, others without confessing or receiving the last sacraments. One of them was a prelate, who had injured him deeply. After his death he appeared to the Servant in a vision, and announced that God had cut off his life and his dignities as a punishment, and that he would long languish and suffer as a penance.

The Provincial Minister exonerated him from blame, and said that he and the General of the Order had rigorously investigated it, as was their duty, and had found nothing against him, save that a wicked woman, who could not be trusted, had spoken maliciously against the worthy man, and that it might happen again, if one gave ear to slanderous tongues.[1]

God soon afterwards took away the companion also, who had treated him so churlishly. All obstacles that had separated him from the naked contemplatiom of the divinity had fallen away from him. The companion appeared after his death to the Servant in a shining golden garment, embraced him affectionately and craved forgiveness for the wrong he had done him, asking that a true, heavenly friendship might continue between them for ever.

Later, when it seemed to God that the time had come, the sufferer was compensated by God for all the afflictions he had ever had, by inward peace of mind, calm restfulness and enlightened grace.

[1] This paragraph is only to be found in the Munich manuscript, and may be a later addition.

CHAPTER XXXIX

Of Inner Suffering

WHEN the spiritual daughter had read the above story of sad suffering, and had wept copiously with pity, she asked him to tell her also what was the nature of inner suffering. He said: 'I will tell thee two stories about inner suffering. In a religious Order there was once a nobleman, for whom God had ordained inner suffering, and in this trial the poor friar's heart and soul were so downcast that he went about weeping and wailing and lamenting day and night. The friar came to the Servant of Eternal Wisdom, very devoutly, confided his troubles, and asked the Servant to pray that God would help him. Early one morning, the Servant was praying for him. As he sat in his chapel, he had a vision and saw the Evil One himself come up to him. He appeared in his own shape, as a hideous Moor,[1] with fiery eyes. He had a hellish and dreadful countenance, and held a bow in his hand. The Servant spoke to him thus: 'I conjure thee by the living God to tell me what thou art, or what thou seekest here.' The devil said in a diabolical voice: 'I am the spirit of blasphemy, and thou shalt know soon enough what I desire.'

The Servant turned round to the door of the choir. Then the suffering friar entered the door, and was about to go into the choir to hear Mass. But the evil spirit drew his bow, and shot a fiery arrow into the friar's heart, so that he fell down backwards, and could not enter the choir. This troubled the Servant, and he reprimanded the devil severely for it. For this reason the devil became angry with him, and he drew his bow with a fiery

[1] A mediæval tradition.

arrow as before, and he would have shot him also in the heart. But the Servant turned swiftly to Our Lady for help, saying: 'Nos cum prole pia benedicat virgo Maria.'[1] The devil's strength deserted him, and he disappeared from sight. When the day dawned, he told the suffering friar about it. The Servant comforted him, telling him what alone would help him, as he wrote in one of his sermons: 'Lectulus noster floridus.'[2]

Among the many suffering persons who visited him there was a layman from foreign parts, who said to him: 'Sir, I have the very greatest pain that ever man felt, and no one can help me. Not long ago, I doubted God, and was in such despair that I was on the point of doing away with myself, and destroying myself, body and soul. I was in great distress, and was about to jump into a raging torrent; as I ran along with the intention of drowning myself, I heard a voice above me saying: "Stop, do not inflict a shameful death on thyself. Seek out a Dominican friar." And the voice mentioned the Servant by name, although he had never heard of him before, and added: "He will help thee, and all will be well with thee." He was glad at this, and refrained from taking his own life. He made enquiries about the Servant, and sought him, as he had been told to do. Seeing that this man was so wretched, the Servant turned to him with kind words of comfort. He relieved his heart of its distress, and instructed him what to do, so that by the help of God he never again underwent such temptation.

[1] 'May the pious Virgin Mary, together with her Son, bless us.'

[2] The text of Suso's first sermon, from Song of Solomon, i, 16.

CHAPTER XL

What Sufferings are the Most Useful to Man and the Most Praiseworthy to God

THE saintly daughter asked: 'I should very much like to know what sufferings above all others are the most useful to man and the most praiseworthy to God.' He answered and said: 'Thou shouldst know that there are many kinds of suffering that prepare men and speed them on their way towards salvation, for those who endure them in the right spirit.'

Sometimes God ordains grievous sufferings for a man although he is not to blame. In such trials God either intends to test him, to see how firmly he stands, or what strength he has in himself, as we often read in the Old Testament, or God has in mind His divine praise and glory, as the gospel relates of the man born blind, whom Christ declared to be guiltless, and to whom He restored his sight.[1]

Some sufferings are, however, well deserved, such as those of the robber who was crucified with Christ, and was redeemed by Christ by his sincere conversion to Him, which he underwent in his suffering.[2] Other sufferings are not due to any fault of the person concerned, but he has in him some defect, for which reason God ordains suffering for him. This often happens when God punishes excessive pride, by throwing back a man on himself, with the painful collapse of his arrogance, in a matter of which he may be entirely innocent.

Some sufferings are given by merciful God to men in order that they may be saved from still greater sufferings,

---

[1] John, ix, 1–3.   [2] Luke, xxiii, 42–3.

as happens to those to whom God gives their purgatory here, in the shape of sickness or poverty, or the like, so that they may be free of these things later. Moreover, he lets devilish men torment them so that they may be spared the sight of diabolical apparitions in the hour of death. There are some men who suffer through true fervent love, such as the martyrs, who in their manifold deaths of the body or the soul, would fain show their love of their dear Lord.

One also finds in this world much vain and disconsolate suffering, such as those feel who strive to satisfy the demands of the world in worldly matters. They must needs earn hell by hard suffering, while a man who suffers for God's sake is able to help himself by his sufferings. Then there are some men whom God often warns inwardly that they should turn to Him, for He would fain be their friend, but they resist Him heedlessly. Sometimes God draws them to him by suffering. Wherever they turn and would gladly escape God, He is there with the temporal misfortunes of this world, and he holds them by the hair, so that they cannot escape Him.

Also one finds people who do not suffer at all, save that they cause themselves pain by exaggerating things that are of no importance. For instance, a man heavily laden with grief was once passing a house, when he heard a woman lamenting grievously. He thought: 'Go and comfort this person in her grief!' He entered the house and said: 'Alas, dear lady, what is the cause of your sad lamentation?' She said: 'I have lost a needle, and cannot find it anywhere.' He turned round, and went out, thinking: 'Alas, thou foolish woman, hadst thou but one of my burdens to bear, thou wouldst not weep for the sake of a needle.' In this way, and for all kinds of reasons, many pampered persons cause themselves suffering that is no suffering at all.

But the noblest and best suffering is a Christlike suffering, I mean that which our heavenly Father gave to His only-begotten Son, and also to His dear Friends. This does not mean that any man is altogether free from guilt, save Christ Himself alone, Who never sinned. But Christ showed Himself patient and bore Himself in suffering like a gentle lamb among wolves,[1] and in the same way He gives to some of His dearest friends at times great sufferings, so that we, who are free from suffering, may learn from these blessed saints how to be patient, and at all times with a gentle heart to overcome evil with good.

All this thou shouldst consider, my daughter, and thou shouldst not suffer unwillingly, for wherever it comes from, it may be helpful to a man if he can rightly accept everything as coming from God, and carry it back to God, and overcome it with Him.

CHAPTER XLI

How He drew some Loving Hearts from Earthly Love to Divine Love

AT this time, when the Servant was earnestly endeavouring to draw men from temporal love to God, he noticed that in some convents there were persons who wore the religious habit, but had wordly hearts beneath it.

Among them there was a young woman who had firmly fixed her heart on that kind of fleeting love which they call 'amorous dalliance', which is a poison to spiritual happiness. So he said to her that if she wished to lead a peaceful, godly life, she should give it up, and take

[1] Luke, x, 3.

Eternal Wisdom as her love instead of her paramour. This was very hard for her to do, for she was young and fresh, and ensnared in such company. Once he brought her to the point that she made up her mind to do so, but her companions dissuaded her. Then he said to her: 'Daughter, give it up! I tell thee, if thou dost not do so willingly, thou wilt do it against thy will.' As she would not follow his friendly advice, he earnestly prayed to God for her, that He would save her from her bad ways, either by joy or sorrow. One day he went, as was his custom, into the pulpit, under the crucifix, and inflicted such a hard discipline on his naked back that the blood ran down, and he prayed to God that she might be brought to her senses. And this came to pass, for when she returned home, an ugly hump suddenly grew on her back, so that she was deformed, and had of necessity to give up what she had refused to give up for the sake of Christ.

In the same open convent[1] there was a young, beautiful high-born girl, who was caught in the net of the devil. For many years she had spent her heart and her time in vanity with all kinds of company. She had become so deluded by them that she always fled from the Servant like a wild animal, fearing that he would forbid her to follow the life she led. Now the sister of this girl entreated him to make an attempt, and see whether he could not bring her to God and draw her away from her harmful life. This seemed to him an impossible request, and he said that it appeared to him more likely that the heavens would fall than that she would give it up, unless death compelled her to do so. But she begged and besought him, and said that she believed that God would not refuse him anything that he earnestly asked for. With such words she persuaded him to promise to do it.

[1] A convent of Beguines, (lay sisters, not bound by vows).

She fled from him at all times, and he could not have speech with her, but he noticed once, about St. Margaret's Day,[1] that she had gone out with the other sisters to a field to pull flax. He slipped out after her, and walked round the field so that he could get near her inconspicuously. When she noticed that he was approaching, she turned her back on him very rudely, and with an angry, fiery face she called out to him vehemently in these words: 'Sir friar, what do you want of me? Take my advice, go your ways! Look, I would rather have my head cut off than confess to you. I would rather be buried alive than obey you, and give up keeping company with men. So go your ways, for you will have no success with me!'

Her companion, who was standing nearest to her, silenced her and scolded her, saying that he had only acted for the best. She tossed her head angrily, and said: 'Look, I will be frank with him; I will show him with words and deeds what I have in my mind!' At her insolent words and unseemly gestures the Servant was horrified; flushing with shame, he was silent, and could not speak. Going quickly to one side, he turned away from her. He looked up, sighing deeply, and wishing to have nothing more to do with her, but an inner impulse from God remained with him, and said: 'He who intends to achieve anything with God or with the world, should not give up so soon!' This happened in the afternoon.

When the evening came, the sisters were going together after the evening meal into the courtyard, to ripple the flax. The girl went with them, and they had to pass the guest-house, where the Servant was staying. So he asked one of her companions to bring this girl to him on some pretext, and then to go away. With some difficulty she managed to do this.

[1] 15th July.

[*134*]

The girl came in, and sat down below the window beside him. He then spoke to her, sighing deeply from the depths of his heart, saying: 'Ah, fair, gentle maiden chosen by God, how long will you allow your beautiful, lovely body and your tender lovely heart to belong to the foul fiend? You are so graciously formed by God in your person, and it is a great misfortune that such an angel, such a handsome, noble woman should belong to anyone else as a lover than to the Noblest of all. Who has a better claim to pluck the fair, gentle rose than He to Whom it belongs? No, dear, lovely maiden, open your clear falcon's eyes, and remember the fair love that begins here and lasts for ever. And consider also, what grief and infidelity, pain and sorrow, in body, possessions and reputation, those must endure, whether they will or no, who act as you do, unless the sweet poison so beguiles them that they forget for a moment the great loss that follows them in time and eternity.[1] Ah, therefore, angelic vision, thou lovely noble heart, turn thy natural nobility to Him Who is eternally noble, and give it up! By my faith, I promise that God will have thee as His love, and will show thee complete fidelity and true love, here and in heaven for ever.'

The hour was favourable. These fiery words pierced her heart, and calmed her to such an extent that she raised her eyes swiftly, heaving a profound sigh, and said from the very depths of her being, with bold brave words: 'Ah, sir and father, I surrender myself this day to God and to you. From this hour I bid freely farewell to my vain, depraved life, and according to your counsel and with your help, I will give myself to God to be His own child, and will serve Him only until I die.' He said: 'This is a happy hour. Praised be God in His mercy Who

[1] Note the change of pronoun here, from the respectful *you* to the familiar *thou*.

[135]

will joyfully receive all those who return to Him!'

While these two were talking together in this way about God, her frivolous companions were standing outside the door. They were annoyed at the length of the conversation, fearing that she would renounce their worldly society. They called on her to stop. She stood up a new person, went out to them, and exclaimed: 'My friends, may God bless you! I bid you all farewell, both you and all your companions, with whom I have, alas, wasted my time, for now I will belong to God alone, and let everything else go.'

The girl began to avoid all harmful society, and to keep herself apart. However much they tried to win her back to the old manner of life, it was of no avail. She bore herself in such a way that she remained firm and steadfast in praiseworthy conduct and divine virtues before God until her death.

Once afterwards, the Servant went out to confirm his new daughter in the good life, and to comfort her kindly if she was in any grief, and he brought pain upon himself because of the illness with which he was then afflicted. As he walked through the deep mire, and climbed up the high mountains, he often raised up his eyes to God and said: 'Merciful God, be mindful of the painful footsteps Thou didst tread for the sake of man's salvation, and preserve my child!' His companion, on whom he always leaned, said with pity: 'It accords well with God's goodness that many a soul should be saved through you.'

When he had gone on until he could go no further, and was quite exhausted, his companion said: 'Ah, father, God should indeed consider your illness, and send you a pony, so that you can ride on it until you come to human habitations.' He answered: 'Now that we have both prayed, I trust that God will reward thy virtue, and that it may come to pass.' So the Servant looked round,

and saw there on the right hand a beautiful pony, well
saddled and bridled, coming out of the wood towards
them. His companion cried with joy: 'Ah, dear father,
look and you will see that God will not abandon you!'
He said: 'Look, son, all round this broad field, to see if
there is anyone accompanying it, to whom it belongs.'
He looked in every direction, and saw no one but the
pony trotting towards them. So he said: 'Father, in truth
God has sent it to you; mount and ride.' The Servant
said: 'Look, friend, if the pony stops when it comes to us,
I will believe that God has sent it here for our need.' The
pony came gently, and stood still before them. He said:
'Welcome in God's name.' His companion helped him
into the saddle and let him ride, and walked beside him
for some distance, until he had had a rest. When they
drew near to a village, he dismounted, put the bridle once
more on the pony's neck, and bade it go the way it had
come. Whither it then went, or to whom it belonged, he
was never able to find out afterwards.

When the Servant had reached the place for which he
was bound, it chanced one evening that he was sitting
with his spiritual daughters, and was telling them of the
evils of fleeting love, and extolling eternal love. When
they left him, his heart was, so to speak, inflamed with
divine love. For he thought that his Love that he loved,
and urged others to love, was far better than all the loves
of this world. And during his meditation he fell into a
trance, and it seemed to him in a vision that he was being
led to a fair green meadow, and a noble heavenly youth
was walking beside him, holding him by the hand. Then
the youth struck up a song, and it sounded so joyous that
all the Servant's senses were enraptured through the
power of the sweet melody.

When the song was over, a picture was drawn for him,
in which the angels strove to teach him the melody, lest

he should forget it. So he looked at it and saw Our Lady, holding her Child, Eternal Wisdom, clasped to her maternal heart. Now the beginning of the song was written over the Child's head in beautiful ornamental letters, and the writing was so secret that not everyone could read it. Only those persons who had achieved insight by extreme sensitiveness read it easily. The writing ran: *Herzenstrut*.[1] The Servant read the writing quickly, and then he looked at the Child lovingly, and he felt how true it is that He alone is the gentle *Herzenstrut,* in Whom we have joy without sorrow, and he pressed Him to his heart, and then he struck up and sang the song right through, with the youth. And in this fervent heartfelt love, he came to himself, and found his right hand lying on his heart, as he had laid it there to solace it in his stormy emotions.

Once he had walked so far that he was tired, and in the evening he came to a convent in a strange town, where they[2] intended to stay the night. There was no wine there, neither in the town nor in the convent, but a kind-hearted girl came out, and said she had a small bottle of wine, about a pint, but 'what help would that be among so many people?' for there were some twenty persons among those who had come thither, desiring to hear the word of God preached from his mouth. He ordered the little bottle to be brought in and put on the table, and they begged him to say grace over it. And he did so in the powerful strength of the beloved name of Jesus, and he drank first, for he was thirsty after the journey. Then he offered it to them, and they all drank together. The bottle was put down before them, in the sight of everyone, and no water or wine was added to it, for there was no more wine there. But they drank again and again out of the same bottle, and were so desirous to hear the word

[1] Beloved of my heart.   [2] Suso and his companion.

of God from him that no one heeded the divine miracle. At last, when they had come to themselves, and they saw so clearly the powerful strength of God in the increase of the drink, they began to praise God, and wanted to attribute it to the holiness of the Servant. He refused to allow it, and said: 'Children, this is not my work. God has rewarded the pious company for their true faith, and has strengthened them physically and spiritually.'

CHAPTER XLII

Of Certain Suffering Persons Who were attached to the Servant with Particular Affection

IN a certain town there were two persons of outstanding holiness who were his intimate friends. The ways of these two Friends of God were very different. One of them was of high rank in the world, and was endowed with divine joy; the other was not of noble birth, and God tried her continually with suffering. When they died, the Servant wanted to know of God what different rewards they received in the other world, since in this world they had led such different lives. Early one morning, one of them appeared to him, the one who was so aristocratic, and told him that she was still in purgatory. When he asked how this was possible, she said she had incurred no guilt, except that, as a result of her noble birth, spiritual pride had risen up in her, and she had not suppressed it quickly enough. But her sufferings would soon be at an end. The other one, who had been an afflicted suffering soul, went straight to God without hindrance.

The Servant's mother was also a great sufferer all her

days. The cause was the unfortunate difference between her and her husband. She was full of God, and accordingly would fain have lived spiritually. But he was full of the world, and opposed her with harsh severity, and hence came much suffering. She was accustomed to cast all her cares on the bitter sufferings of Christ, and thus she overcame her own trials. She confessed to her son before her death that for over thirty years she had never gone to Mass without weeping bitterly, with heart-felt sympathy, for the Passion of Our Lord and His faithful Mother. She also told him that, owing to the extreme love she had for God, she once fell sick and lay twelve weeks in bed, so full of sorrow and longing for God that the physicians noticed it, and were much edified thereby.

Once, at the beginning of Lent, she was going into the cathedral, in which the descent from the Cross was represented in carving on one of the altars. And in front of this sculpture, she experienced and felt acutely the great pain that the gentle Mother underwent under the cross. And in her agony, this good lady felt such sorrowful pity that her heart broke as it were, painfully in her body, so that she fell to the ground in a swoon, and could neither see nor speak. When she had been helped home, she lay sick until Good Friday at none, and then she died as the Passion was being read.[1]

At this time her son, the Servant, was studying in Cologne, and she appeared to him in a vision and said with great joy: 'Ah, my child, love God and trust in Him; He will by no means desert thee in any adversity. Look, I have departed from this world, and yet I am not dead. I am to live eternally in the presence of God.' She kissed him maternally on the mouth, and blessed him affectionately and disappeared. He began to weep, and called after her: 'Alas, faithful one, my saintly mother, remem-

[1] From the Gospel of the day.

[*140*]

ber me before God!' And he came to himself again, weeping and sighing.

In his young days, when he went to school, God once provided him with a dear godly companion. One day, in a confidential talk, when they had conversed much of God, his companion begged him by his loyal friendship to show him and let him see the beloved name of Jesus inscribed on his heart. The Servant was unwilling to do so, but in the face of so great a devotion, he granted the request, and opened his garment over his heart, and let him see the precious emblem as much as he desired. This did not suffice for his companion. When he had seen it clearly on the Servant's body, right over his heart, he put his hand upon it and stroked it, and put his mouth on it. He wept deeply with devotion, so that his flowing tears ran down over the heart. Then the Servant concealed the name, and would never allow any person to see it, save one chosen Friend of God, to whom permission was given by God. He also looked at it with the same devotion as the other.

When the two companions had spent several years together in pious friendship, and had to separate, they blessed each other, and made a mutual compact that if one of them died first, he would be faithful to the other after his death, and say two Masses for him for a year, a Requiem Mass on Mondays and a Mass of our Lord's Passion on Fridays. Then many years later, the Servant's companion died, and the Servant had forgotten his promise to say Masses for him, but he faithfully remembered his companion in other respects. One morning, as he was sitting lost in meditation in his chapel, his companion came to him in a vision, stood before him, and said: 'My friend, alas for thy unfaithfulness! How hast thou forgotten me!' The Servant said: 'I remember thee every day in my Mass.' The companion said: 'It is not enough. Fulfil our compact concerning the masses, so that the innocent blood[1] may flow down upon me, and so that this fierce fire may be extinguished, and then I shall be immediately released from purgatory.' And the Servant did so in loyal friendship, with great grief for his forgetfulness; and his companion was helped at once.

CHAPTER XLIII

How Christ appeared to Him in the Shape of a Seraph, and taught Him how to Suffer

ONCE, when the Servant had turned to God with great earnestness, and asked Him to teach him how to suffer, there appeared before him in a spiritual vision the likeness of the crucified Christ in the shape of a seraph; and this angelic seraph had six wings, with two it covered its head, with two its feet, and with two it flew.[2] On the two lowest wings was written: 'Accept suffering willingly'; on the middle ones it said: 'Bear suffering patiently'; and on the two highest ones: 'Learn to suffer after the example of Christ.'

This lovely vision he related to a saintly friend, who was a very holy person. Then she answered: 'Know for certain, that once more God will prepare new sufferings for you that you must endure.' He asked what kind of sufferings they were. She said: 'You must now be raised up to be a prelate, so that those can better strike you who are ill-disposed to you, and that they may the better

[1] The blood of Christ.

[2] Isaiah, vi, 2. St. Francis of Assisi had a similiar vision; see *The Little Flowers of St. Francis,* edited by Thomas Okey, 1912 (Everyman), p. 114.

[*142*]

oppress you. For this reason put on humility, as the Seraph showed you to do.' He sighed and looked out for a new storm in the future. And indeed it happened as the saintly woman had predicted.

It came to pass in those days that there was a famine,[1] and in the friary in which he lived there was neither bread nor wine, and the friary had got deeply into debt. The assembled friars agreed that in the great scarcity they should elect the Servant as their prior, unpleasant and distasteful as it was to him, for he well understood that new sufferings were impending.

The first day he ordered the bell to be rung to summon the chapter, and urged them to call upon St. Dominic, for the saint had promised to his brethren that when they called upon him in their distress he would come to their help. Two friars were sitting together in the chapter; one of them whispered to the other scornfully: 'Look, what a foolish man this prior is! He tells us to turn to God in our distress! Does he think that God will open the heavens and send us food and drink out of them?' The other said: 'Not only is he a fool, we are all fools together for electing him, since we all knew before that he does not concern himself with temporal things, and does nothing but gape up at the sky.' Many such scornful judgments were expressed about him.

When morning came, he ordered a Mass of St. Dominic to be sung, so that he might help them. As he was meditating in his place in the choir, the porter came to him, and called him out to a rich canon, who was his particular friend. The latter said to him: 'Dear sir, you are not acquainted with worldly things, and last night I was inwardly admonished by God to help you in His place. Here I am bringing you twenty pounds in

[1] This was in 1343–4; it is mentioned in the Chronicle of Johannes Vitorodanus.

Constance *Pfennige,* as a first instalment. Have faith in God: He will not desert you.' The Servant was glad, and accepted the money, and ordered bread and wine to be bought. And God and St. Dominic helped him as long as he was prior, so that there was a plentiful supply of everything. He also paid off all their debts.

This canon of whom we have spoken, when he lay on his deathbed, bequeathed large sums of money to good causes to which he was devoted, to be spent on Masses and alms for his soul. Then he sent for the Servant, who was then prior, and handed over to him many florins to be distributed elsewhere, among poor Friends of God, who had consumed their strength by severe austerities. The Servant did not wish to do this, fearing subsequent suffering, as also came to pass. Finally he was persuaded to accept the money, and he journeyed forth into the country, and distributed the money, as he had promised to do, in various places, as would be most helpful for the canon's soul. He acted with the greatest care, and rendered an account to his superiors. Thereupon he fell into great sufferings.

The canon had an ill-mannerly illegitimate son, who had wasted what his father had given him, and in his ruthlessness had fallen into evil ways. He very much wanted to have the money, and as he could not get it, he vowed vengeance on the Servant, and swore a solemn oath that he would kill him wherever he came across him. No one could put a stop to this dangerous enmity, often as it was attempted. The man only wanted to kill the Servant. The poor man was in fear and anguish for a long time, not daring to walk to and fro, from fear of being murdered by his unscrupulous enemy. He raised up his eyes to God, and said with a deep sigh: 'Ah, God, what a miserable death is this that Thou wilt ordain for me.' His distress was all the greater because not long before a

[*144*]

friar had been foully murdered under similar circumstances. The poor friar had no one who was able or who dared to protect him in his distress, because of the cruelty of the savage man. But he approached the Highest Lord in the matter, Who saved him from his foe, and broke off the young life of the latter so that he died.

To this trial was added another bitter grief. There was a whole parish to which the canon had given generously. They were, however, not satisfied, but fell upon the friar with great hostility, accusing him of withholding some of the money from them. Hence he was cruelly persecuted by them; the news was brought to the secular and ecclesiastical courts, and was spread far abroad in distorted form. Thus he fell in the estimation of people in matters of which, in the eyes of God, he was innocent. When this painful affair had been silenced for a time, it was revived again and again. This continued for years, until the poor man was nearly distracted by it.

About this time the dead canon appeared to him in a vision. He had on a beautiful garment which was green, and was covered with roses all over. And he told the Servant that it was well with him in the other world, and bade him endure patiently the great injustice that was imposed upon him, for God would recompense him well for it all. He asked the canon what his beautiful clothing signified. He said: 'The roses in the green field, that is your patient suffering; you have clothed me in them, and God will clothe you both here and with Himself in eternity.'

CHAPTER XLIV

How Firmly He must contend Who would win the Spiritual Prize

In the inexperience of his beginning, the Servant felt a hearty wish to be well-pleasing in the eyes of his beloved God by noble distinction, but without suffering or toil. It once happened that he was travelling in the country for the purpose of preaching. He had embarked on an ordinary ship on the Lake of Constance, and among the other passengers sitting there, was a valiant squire, who wore fashionable clothing. The Servant went up to him and asked whose vassal he was.

He answered: 'I am a squire in search of adventure, and I gather the knights together for festive occasions, when they fight with lances and in tournaments, and serve their fair ladies. And the one who excels in this, to him is given the honour and reward.' The Servant said: 'What is the reward?' The squire answered: 'The fairest lady present puts a golden ring on his finger.' He asked again: 'Tell me, friend, what must one do, in order to obtain the honour and the ring?' He said: 'He who endures the most blows and attacks and does not quail, but bears himself valiantly and manfully, he who sits firm in the saddle and lets blows rain upon him: such men gain the prize.' He asked again: 'Ah, tell me, would it be enough for a man to be brave in the first attack?' He said: 'No, he must endure right through the tournament, and if he is struck so hard that the sparks are struck from his eyes, and the blood bursts from his mouth and nose, he must suffer all this, if he is to win praise.' He asked again: 'Ah, my friend, dare he weep or bear himself disconsolately if he is struck hard?' He said: 'No, even if his heart quails

[*146*]

within his body, as happens to many, he dare not show it. He must bear himself cheerfully and valiantly, otherwise he is an object of mockery, and loses the honour and the ring.'

At these words the Servant was depressed; he sighed from the depths of his heart, and said: 'Ah, Lord God, the knights of this world must suffer such pains and for such slight reward, which in itself is nothing! Ah, God, how fitting it is that men should suffer much more for an eternal prize! Ah, fair, lovely Eternal Wisdom, to whose graciousness there is no equal in all lands, if but a ring might be vouchsafed to my soul from Thee, Ah, I would suffer for it whatever Thou didst desire!'

When he arrived at the town to which he was going, God sent him such great and manifest sufferings that the poor man almost lost his faith in God, and many an eye was wet with pity for him. He had forgotten all his chivalrous valour, and the promises he had made to God, when his mind was bent on spiritual chivalry. He became wretched and rebellious against God, asking himself what charge God had brought against him, and why He had sent him such great sufferings. When the day dawned, a calm spread over his soul, and in an ecstasy, he heard a voice speak to him thus: 'Where now are thy noble chivalry and thy vows? What is the good of a knight of straw and a man of cloth? To be very valiant in joy, and then to give up in sorrow, is this the way to win the eternal ring that thou dost desire?' He answered and said: 'Alas, Lord, the tournaments in which one must suffer for Thy sake are much too arduous.' An answer came to him: 'But the praise and glory, and the ring of My knights, who are honoured by Me, are steadfast and eternal.' Then the Servant was downcast, and said very humbly: 'Lord, I am wrong, permit me to weep alone in my sufferings, for my heart is so very full.' He said: 'Woe

[147]

to thee, wilt thou weep like a woman? Thou art disgraced in the heavenly court! Wipe thy eyes, and bear thyself cheerfully, so that neither God nor man may observe that thou hast wept because of thy sufferings.' He began to laugh, and yet the tears fell at the same time, down over his cheeks, and he promised to God that he would weep no longer, in order that the spiritual ring might be given to him by God.

CHAPTER XLV

Of the Beloved Name of Jesus

THE Servant of Eternal Wisdom was once travelling from the mountains to Aachen, to visit Our Lady there. When he returned, Our Lady appeared to a very saintly person[1] and said to her: 'Look, the Servant of my Child has come, and spread the love of the sweet name of Jesus far and wide, as formerly His disciples spread it. Just as they wished to make this name known to all men, together with the faith, in the same way he endeavours with great enthusiasm to kindle the name of Jesus in all cold hearts. For this he shall receive eternal reward with them, after his death.' Thereupon the same holy person looked at Our Lady and saw that she was holding a fair candle in her hand, which burnt so beautifully that it shone throughout the world, and round and round the candle was written the name *Jesus*. Then Our Lady spoke to the person: 'Look, this burning candle signifies the name of Jesus, for He truly illuminates all hearts that devoutly accept His name, and honour Him and carry about with them the love of Him. And my Child has chosen the Servant for Himself, to the end that through

[1] Elsbeth Stagel.

[*148*]

him His name may be kindled through love in many hearts and that they may be led to eternal bliss.'

When this saintly woman noticed in many ways that her spiritual father had such great devotion and firm faith in the lovely name of Jesus, which he bore on his heart, she acquired a special love of it, and she devoutly sewed this name of Jesus in red silk on a small piece of cloth, in this form: IHS, which she intended to wear herself secretly. She also made countless copies of it and brought it about that the Servant wore all these names next to his heart, and she sent them to various places to his spiritual daughters, with a spiritual blessing. It was made known to her by God that if anyone wore the name on him, and said a Paternoster daily in his honour, God would be gracious to him in this life, and would give him aid at his latter end.

With such strict austerities and with the divine example of Jesus Christ and His dear Friends, this saintly woman began her religious life.

Epilogue

THE saintly maiden had been instructed by her spiritual father in all Christian truth with careful explanations, and had been taught all the ways that lead to true blessedness. She fully understood everything, as far as is possible in this world. He then wrote to her in his last letter, among other things: 'Now, daughter, bid farewell to all creatures, and cease from asking questions; listen to what God speaks within thee. Thou hast reason to rejoice that it has been given to thee to know what is hidden from many, and however hard the learning of it has been, it is all over now, in the fullness of time. Nothing now remains, save to dwell in divine peace, and in quiet rest and joy to abide the hour when thou wilt pass from this world to perfect bliss.'

Soon after, it came to pass that the maiden died,[1] and had a blessed end, just as all her life had been blessed. After her death, she appeared to her spiritual father in a supernatural vision, shining in a snow-white garment, adorned with bright light, and full of heavenly joy. She came to him and revealed to him how nobly she had become one with the pure Godhead. He saw and heard this with happiness and joy, and his soul was full of divine comfort through this vision. When he came to himself, he sighed deeply and thought: 'Ah, God, how happy are those who strive for Thee alone. They can gladly bear their sorrows, if Thou wilt thus reward them. May God help us to rejoice in this saintly maiden and in all the dear Friends of God, and may we be permitted to contemplate His face eternally.' Amen.

[1] In the year 1360.